Life in the Shadows

A Story of Resilience

Kathleen Geuder Martin

LIFE IN THE SHADOWS
A Story of Resilience

Library of Congress Control Number: 2023909261
ISBN: 978-1-949053-17-3

Designed by
Beth Foster, Pinecone Book Company

Books available from bookstores
and from Kady Martin
13860 W. 67 Ct.
Arvada, CO 80004

Other Works by Kathleen (Kady) Martin
Party Shakers (children's book)
Let's Party (family book)
I Hate To Wait (children's book)
Tell a Tale (children's participatory video)

This book is for my sister, Elaine,
and my brother, Richard. We are survivors.

Elaine, Richard and Kathleen

Momma's Family Tree

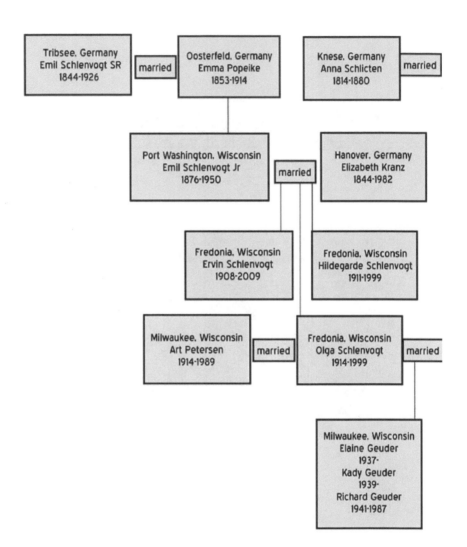

Tribsee, Germany
Emil Schlenvogt SR
1844-1926

married

Oosterfeld, Germany
Emma Popeike
1853-1914

Knese, Germany
Anna Schlicten
1814-1880

married

Port Washington, Wisconsin
Emil Schlenvogt Jr
1876-1950

married

Hanover, Germany
Elizabeth Kranz
1844-1982

Fredonia, Wisconsin
Ervin Schlenvogt
1908-2009

Fredonia, Wisconsin
Hildegarde Schlenvogt
1911-1999

Milwaukee, Wisconsin
Art Petersen
1914-1989

married

Fredonia, Wisconsin
Olga Schlenvogt
1914-1999

married

Milwaukee, Wisconsin
Elaine Geuder
1937-
Kady Geuder
1939-
Richard Geuder
1941-1987

Dad's Family Tree

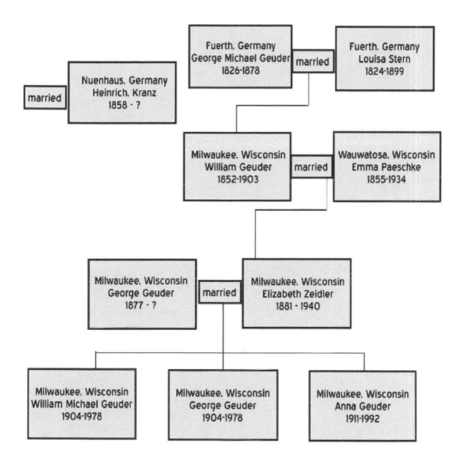

married

Nuenhaus, Germany
Heinrich, Kranz
1858 - ?

Fuerth, Germany
George Michael Geuder
1826-1878

married

Fuerth, Germany
Louisa Stern
1824-1899

Milwaukee, Wisconsin
William Geuder
1852-1903

married

Wauwatosa, Wisconsin
Emma Paeschke
1855-1934

Milwaukee, Wisconsin
George Geuder
1877 - ?

married

Milwaukee, Wisconsin
Elizabeth Zeidler
1881 - 1940

Milwaukee, Wisconsin
William Michael Geuder
1904-1978

Milwaukee, Wisconsin
George Geuder
1904-1978

Milwaukee, Wisconsin
Anna Geuder
1911-1992

"You can't control the wind, but you can adjust your sails."
Yiddish Proverb

"There is no greater agony than bearing an untold story inside you."
Maya Angelou

"We live in a world that normalizes physical health
but stigmatizes mental health challenges."
Author Unknown

"If you see the moon, you will see the beauty of God.
If you see the sun, you will see the power of God.
If you see a mirror, you will see God's best creation. So, believe it!"
Charlie Chaplin

"I now know how little I know about what I want to know."
Kady Martin

Table of Contents

Prologue
Unlocking the Secret

I have a secret. I didn't know it was a secret. Why was it a secret? Maybe because we never spoke about it. I don't remember my siblings and I ever discussing it. We lived with it. It was the elephant in the room. No one thinks it's there, but it's there—waiting to be acknowledged. It hurts to think about it. If anyone knew, what would they think of us? We were too ashamed to reveal the truth. The secret stuck in our throats. We wouldn't let it out.

I was seven years old when it started. My sister Elaine was nine, and our little brother Richard (always called Dick) was six.

Relatives knew, but they never addressed it. Maybe folks whispered behind our backs. God, even my high school friends knew, but they never said anything. I discovered this at my ten-year high school reunion—I detected no *schadenfreude* there.

Why is it that some stories are told over and over again like on a long-playing reel and others are never told at all?

Why are some parts of family stories glossed over, hiding carbuncles and unsightly warts?

How would it feel to emerge from the shadows?

Chapter 1

A Stranger in the Kitchen

In movies and novels, darkening skies, pounding thunder and howling winds generally mean trouble ahead. No one checked the weather that night—maybe it was one of those hot, sticky Milwaukee summer evenings—when a calamity blew in our back door, sucking tranquility out the windows. Minutes before, our life had been filled with giggles. Now we wore the expression of guppies gasping for air.

My siblings and I were playing in the back room. I was gingerly managing my cut-outs, staying within the lines. Elaine was nose deep in a Nancy Drew book. Dick was setting up his toy soldiers on the floor. Suddenly, the sound of a crazed voice blasted through the closed door.

"I'm telling you, someone poisoned my beer!" the voice raged at my mother.

Momma's voice quivered as she tried desperately to control the situation. "What are you talking about, Bill?"

Bam! His fist hit the kitchen table. "I told you, Olga, some son of a bitch, they poisoned my beer!" His body slammed into the chairs, knocking one over. He staggered around the kitchen threatening, shouting. He stomped back and forth, his fists pounding the table. *Bam! Bam!*

My siblings and I tiptoed to the door, opening it a crack. Fear grabbed our bodies. Stomachs churning, my brother and I huddled under our older sister's protective wing. We saw that the madman, eyes bulging, appeared to be our father. He had the same tall, slim build, but that twisted, snarly expression was one we had never seen.

His malevolent face contained eyes like hard black marbles. His body swayed back and forth, unable to walk in a straight line. He yelled, "God damn it! I told you when I went to the bathroom and came back my beer was switched! It was poisoned!" His fists slammed the table and pummeled the backs of the chairs.

As he came closer to Momma, she backed into the wall, hands shaking as she held them up for protection.

Who would want to poison Dad, we wondered? He worked at a candle factory where beer was allowed at lunchtime. After all, Milwaukee, Wisconsin was the beer capital of the world!

"Who would poison Daddy?" I squeaked to my sister.

"Shh!" Elaine put her finger to her lips, her brown eyes wide in fear.

"Bill," Momma pleaded, her voice trembling. "Stop pacing. Sit down. What are you trying to tell me?" She tried placating, pushing a chair toward him.

"God damn it, Olga! I was poisoned. Don't you ever listen?" Spit flying from his mouth, he turned and jerked away from Momma. He stumbled down the back stairs, slamming the door on his way out.

Picking up the phone that sat in a hallway alcove, Momma shut herself in the bathroom and called the family doctor.

Dad returned, thundering through the back door. The door bounced off its hinges, and he crashed into the kitchen wall, rhythmically slamming his fists together and shouting, almost pleading, "Someone poisoned my beer!" Crying desperately for help like a wounded animal caught in a snare, he flopped into the remaining upright chair, where he sat holding his head in his hands, whimpering.

"What's happening?" we wondered.

Clutching each other's arms, my siblings and I stumbled over to the large pink chair in the corner and crammed our stiff bodies into it, tears streaming down our faces, praying we wouldn't be found.

Over and over, I prayed, "Please, God, help us."

After what seemed like an eternity, Dr. Torre arrived. He didn't even ring the doorbell; he just rushed right in.

Between Dad's crazy rages, the doctor worked to ascertain the problem. His voice was calm as he tried to soothe our out-of-control father. Dad shouted, "Take my pee and analyze it! There's poison in it!"

The doctor listened intently, trying to calm Dad. There was no consoling him nor trying to decipher what had transpired. Maybe the doctor told Dad they would take a urine sample at the hospital; I don't know.

The police were called. I don't think they rang the doorbell either, just marched right into the kitchen. One cop grabbed my father's left arm and the other cop his right. "Let go of me!" Dad yelled. "Leave me alone! Get away from me! No! You can't take me anywhere! Let me go!" He was now shouting like his life depended on it.

They dragged him out the front door and down the steps to the squad car, his feet barely touching the ground. He was screaming like a frightened child. "No! No! Let me go!" he cried out. They pushed him into the back seat and sped down Wisconsin Avenue.

I flung open the window and screamed bloody murder. "Don't hurt my daddy! Let him go! You're hurting him! No! Stop! Let him go! Stop it!" Tears poured from my eyes. I was shrieking like a banshee. "Stop hurting him! Bring him back! Don't hurt his arms! STOP!"

Only minutes before I had been praying for someone to help us. Now I was screaming at them to let my father go. Children—unconditional love comes pouring forth.

Dad was taken to the Milwaukee County Hospital. Momma told us the doctors would give him a mental examination. We had no idea what that meant; we just knew something was different, something was very wrong, and we hoped the doctor would fix him.

After the doctor left, Momma came into the back room, her ashen face reflecting what had just unfolded in a matter of minutes. She told us our father had had a nervous breakdown. He would stay at the hospital to get well. Her hands were wrapping and unwrapping a tear-soaked tissue. That strong, solid woman looked so small and frail, her mind absorbing the shock of her life. She returned to the kitchen and sat down, face in her hands, sobbing loudly. We gathered around her, wishing we could all disappear. How would we remedy this mad situation? We were caught like fireflies in a jar, our lights extinguished.

Somewhere that evening, children were being tucked into their beds; loving fathers pushing back their hair, kissing their foreheads. Somewhere in the world, children were wondering what had happened to their vanquished families. Could there have been families experiencing the same horror we were? On Wisconsin Avenue in 1947, three sorrowful children huddled together in one bed, holding hands, silently praying, "Please, God, make this nightmare disappear."

Chapter 2

Life's Gossamer Veil Removed

Dad was gone for a week. Each day we shook off a little of the terror we had witnessed. There was a sense of ease, a lightness—yet something was amiss. My stomach was tied in knots. (I've always found the stomach an accurate gauge of impending trouble.)

The air was filled with tension. You had the feeling someone was going to lurch out at you … perhaps someone around the next corner. Maybe someone is hiding in the coalbin, waiting to grab you as you race to fetch a jar of jam from the fruit cellar. I would stand at the top of the basement stairs, turn the light on, and run like the wind to the fruit cellar and back, never daring a glance at the dark coalbin. Thinking gratefully, "Whew, no one got me!"

The kitchen episode removed life's gossamer veil. The illusions of a fairytale life were gone, to be savored only in books. Ozzie-and-Harriet lifestyles aren't real. Not every person is born healthy. We learned at a young age that life could change abruptly. Our minds were more alert, preparing for the unexpected.

Momma was quiet, pensive, her mind filled with anguish, her life now changed. How was she going to untangle this new reality? A developing wretched awareness had to be confronted.

I know we were good kids—keeping out of her way, playing outside, not seeking attention. But the ground we stood on was cracked and shaky.

When I was in second grade—I must have been about seven—we learned that the earth is a ball. What? This revelation startled me. They never told us what the earth looked like in Sunday school. I remember walking home from school that day singing, "We live on a ball. I hope I never fall off this little blue ball." I felt like a character from my favorite Moffat book, dropping down to peer between my legs and take a different look at the world upside-down. I wondered why the trees didn't fall over. Life seemed very mysterious!

I think I liked life better before I discovered so many facts. Maybe it was easier not to know everything. Like the saying, "Ignorance is bliss." What other secrets were waiting to reveal themselves?

On Saturday we awoke to the warm smell of freshly baked bread. Mmm ... the inviting aroma curled around our noses, awakening hunger in our empty bellies. I jumped out of bed, rushing to find my play clothes. (Play clothes, that is so funny! They were our everyday clothes except for our Sunday best.)

Pushing open the kitchen door, I saw Momma pounding bread dough. *Bam, bam,* punching the dough over and over. There were pans of rising bread dough on the kitchen table, covered with a blue-striped cloth. One shiny brown crusty loaf was cooling on the table in the back hall. I've often thought making bread is a good deterrent to anxiety. Punching the dough releases tension from one's body.

"What is all this bread for?" I asked Momma. She didn't answer. Just thump, thump, thump, punch, punching the dough on the breadboard and back into waiting beige bowls. Her eyes lingered on something invisible.

My siblings and I wondered if we had slept through breakfast. Finally, she turned and realized we were standing there. "Grab a bowl and make yourself some breakfast," she said distractedly.

We didn't question her. We filled our bowls high with Wheaties, not bickering over who would get the coveted mask on the back of the empty cereal box. We knew this was not the time to argue among ourselves. Just fill the bowl with cereal, pour the dang milk on, and eat it quickly before the Wheaties get soggy. Out the back door we dashed, grabbing a jump rope and some chalk for hopscotch—anything to make a clean getaway.

The week had flown by. No one mentioned Dad or where he was or what was happening to him. We were told he'd had a nervous breakdown and the doctors would fix him. That seemed like a reasonable explanation. You're sick, you go to the doctor, the doctor fixes you. We didn't question it.

Just as we escaped into the back yard, we heard the front doorbell ring. We returned inside.

My Uncle George, dad's twin brother, entered through the front door with Dad lagging behind him. "Here's your dad, kids; come and say hello," he beamed. Uncle George was the most devoted brother. He and Dad often seemed like they were joined at the hip.

Momma rushed into the living room, wiping her hands on her cherry-red apron. "Bill, Bill!" she cried. "You're back!" Dad sat down in a chair near to the door. Momma plunked herself into his lap, threw her arms around his neck, and told him how good he looked, how happy she was to see him. A smile illuminated her face.

We kids were not so sure. The man in the chair looked like our father, but so did that stranger who had appeared in our kitchen. His eyes, though; oh, his eyes spoke volumes. They were frightened, penetrating eyes, like they had seen a monster, the kind of monster that lurks in your closet waiting to grab you. Years later we were told he had received electric shock treatments—the treatment that sent your teeth flying (if you had false teeth). We were paralyzed, as if an unseen magnet gripped us in place. We had seen the monster in the kitchen: the raving, screaming person who was our father.

Uncle George, having returned his brother to his family, left. Momma went to the kitchen to brew a pot of coffee. Dad sat silently in his chair. Dick and Elaine crept outside. I was still confused as to what was happening. Did the doctors really fix him? Would he go back to playing the piano? Would we sit beside him belting out, "Mares eat oats and does eat oats and little lambs eat ivy," like we once had? Would he help us dig out a fort in the deep snow in the backyard? Would we have fun raking leaves into a huge pile then jumping and burrowing deep within? Would we carry bushels of leaves to the back field and stand in awe as Dad set the leaves on fire? That acrid smell lingers in my memory, reminding me of happier days.

Would Momma smile again? Would she feel contentment watching Dad working outside, playing with us kids? Would Dad return to working at the candle factory, and could Momma resume her wifely/ motherly tasks? Would we all sing songs while driving in our car with the plush lining? How I was hoping to go back to those days, hanging over the front seat, singing, "Smoke, smoke that cigarette. Smoke, smoke until you're dead" into his ear while he was driving. Was that kitchen episode just a bad dream that would never happen again? I had no way of knowing. The whole world felt insecure.

Real life requires tenacity. The pioneers heading west prepared children for life ahead. The stories they told their children revealed hardships, not fairy godmothers whisking adversity away. It's like the game we played outside, hide and seek. Everyone hides except the seeker, who yells out, "Here I come, ready or not." That's life. You can run, but you cannot hide.

Our lives were not copacetic. They never returned to what I remember as safe. The security blanket had been ripped off. The illusion lasted a week—this good, quiet side of our "different" father. He returned to work, only to come home early the same day, fired. His nerves, we were told, couldn't handle the job. He didn't trust the fellows he worked with in his altered state of mind.

The story we were told again and again was that our father had a nervous breakdown. We soon realized he was also an alcoholic. We accepted these facts. Not until I was in my twenties did I discover that Dad had been diagnosed as paranoid schizophrenic. We were too ashamed to say, "Our father is mentally ill." What would that make us? No one ever mentioned the dreaded words "mentally ill," or "paranoid schizophrenic," and that is how we limped through life. Those frightening words "Our father was diagnosed as paranoid schizophrenic" still stick in my throat. Why is that?

Chapter 3

Shattered Dreams

Dad tried working at other factories with no luck. Each day he returned home with disappointing news: "I was fired."

"Oh, Bill," Momma cried. "You're fired again?" She stood peeling potatoes at the kitchen sink. One potato per person. Dad slowly shuffled into the kitchen, arms dangling at his side. His words hung in the air. Momma turned back, putting the kettle of potatoes on the stove, silently grasping what his situation meant for her, for all of us. Her life was now permanently altered.

Time was Dad's enemy—empty time spent wandering the streets, riding the streetcar. God only knows where he went each day. He felt boxed in. Disillusion swam in his head. A mantra repeated in his snarled brain, that his father's factory had been stolen from him and his twin brother. "Someone stole the formula," was the familiar rant pulsing through his tangled synapses. I used to pray that whoever stole that damn formula would just fess up and return it.

His anger began to mount. There seemed to be no escape from this confusion. Frustrated, angry, he turned into a rancorous person. What was happening? he wondered. How could he stop this madness?

He wasn't alone. I wanted to escape, too. "Momma," I asked, "am I adopted?" Surely there was some mistake and I wasn't part of this crazy family. She just laughed and laughed. I think her hysterical laugh meant we're all in this together. I decided right then and there that all I wanted for graduation was suitcases.

"Bill Bailey, won't you please come home?" That was a popular song at the time. The lyrics included, "I do the cooking, honey; I pay the rent. I'm all alone, won't you please come home?" Maybe Momma wrote it. She gave him money. She had to. He'd ride the streetcar to 27th Street, to a relative's bar. Probably to keep the peace, the relative gave him beers. The jukebox played on and on, song after song. Dad kicked up his heels, whirling round and round the dance floor, grabbing any available partner. When Dad was there, no woman remained alone. If the dance floor felt sticky, off came his shirt, wiping down the floor. His dancing shoes needed to glide across the floor. It was a gay time for Dad and probably for whoever wanted or needed a good dance partner. Two in the morning the bars closed in Milwaukee. Schnockered, he stumbled home.

And then the unexpected happened. A high-pitched primal screaming, sounding like a cornered animal, woke me. My stomach hit my toes. Terror ripped through my body. Jumping out of bed, I raced to the bathroom. There was that strange Dad again, punching Momma in the face. Dad's angry face blazed with hatred, his mouth roaring unintelligible words. His balled-up fists swung and punched at Momma. Hands up defensively, she tried to protect her face.

Momma shrieked, "Bill! Bill! No! Stop it! What is wrong with you?" Tears streamed down her inflamed face; her pink nightgown clung to her body. Towering over her, swinging his fists, Dad roared, "I told you what happened; someone stole the formula from me! God damn it!"

I rushed to Momma's side, my heart held in a viselike grip. I screamed at the top of my lungs: "Stop it! Let my Momma go! Go away, you bad man! Get out of here! Leave her be!" I grabbed onto Momma's waist and kicked at my father. Letting go of Momma, I start pummeling him with my seven-year-old fists.

"Aw, what do you know about it?" he snarled, realizing those pathetic kicks and hits on his backside were from me. "You're just a puppy dog," he scoffed, spittle flying from his curled-up lips. That deep, gravelly voice, a sound I'd never heard before, would haunt me the rest of my life. I still hear it.

"Leave Momma alone!" I shrieked. "Go run away," I screamed at his backside. "Don't you ever come back. Go away FOREVER! I hate you forever and ever and ever."

By some miracle, he did stop punching her. He stumbled away, totally shit-faced, crashing into the walls, teetering off balance, out the kitchen, down the back steps, slamming out the screen door.

Momma couldn't stop crying. She held a wet washcloth to her swollen face. When she went to soak it again in cold water, two black eyes appeared. I kept a tight hold on her waist. Spasmodic sobs erupted from her crinkled-up face. I wanted so much for her sobs to stop.

"He's gone, Momma," I said, leading her to her bed. I crawled in beside her, tears spilling down my face, snot mixing with salty wetness providing a layer of insulation against him. She didn't say a word. What thoughts swirled in her mind, I don't know. I knew the monster in the kitchen had not disappeared. The doctors didn't fix him.

Sleep was not going to happen tonight. Dad reeled back into the house several times, stumbling into the bedroom, shaking his fist over Momma, still bellowing the same nonsense about some damn formula. Momma would wake and cry out, "No, Bill, no!" I screamed louder than she did and told him to get the heck out of here. Noticing me, he left. Where he slept that night is beyond me, and little did I care. I hoped he passed out in the coalbin.

We probably slept a total of two hours. Morning was a somber event. Elaine, Dick and I got up, ate breakfast and, half awake, walked to school. No one felt like talking. What was there to say? We knew our lives had changed, but what could we do about it? It was difficult to reconcile the trauma that had unfolded the night before with the simple act of walking to school.

From that point onward, I never spoke up in school. Too tired from the nights' terror. Later in life I had an opportunity to assist in a classroom. As I sat in the back of the room, overlooking the students, I wondered if any of them had endured a similar trauma the evening before. I remember asking a teacher if she ever wondered what nightmares some of her students might harbor. What their evenings had been like.

She said she did. This was a teacher who understood the uncertainties of life and reached out with love and understanding.

In the evenings, when Dad felt the urge to seek out his relative's bar, he left. Not that he had to frequent that one bar. Milwaukee had bars on every corner and one in the middle of every block. He returned home when the bars closed at two a.m. When his anger mounted at the injustices he imagined had been dealt to him, he drowned his sorrows in pints of beer. Was this an escape from his mental demons? No one knows. No one could stop him, either.

We endured many more such evenings when he lashed out at Momma, his frustrations and anger pouring over her. Each time I heard her wounded cry, I would bolt out of bed, rush to Momma's side, and with the tenacity of a pit bull, pummel the hell out of my father. His churlish, snarling voice churned my stomach into acid. It was as if a fiery dragon had blown through our back door. Boiling with rage, that evil tone of voice sent shivers of hatred through my veins. Who was this person? He'd hover over us, shaking his fist and demanding … what, I don't know. Angry, so very angry. After each episode, I slept with Momma. We were all frazzled to the bone, shuffling through each freakish day.

Then, for some reason, the beatings stopped. Maybe it was because I was always in the bed with Momma when Dad got home. I'll never know. At least that part of our altered life ceased.

When he returned home during the day, slurring his words and pitching back and forth on unsteady feet, I'd fly out the front door with alacrity, down the block to my friends Kabeena and Brenda's white stucco house. Just leaving my home environment made me feel protected. If it was dinner time, I would sit on the wide cement steps of their front porch and wait for them to finish eating. Every so often, I would peek through a window and see this storybook family having dinner. Their very erect father presided at the head of the table; their lovely, graceful, silver-haired mother sat at the other end. The two sisters, on either side of their parents, faced each other. The setting was congenial, with everyone enjoying a sane dinner conversation, as I'm sure many families in Milwaukee were doing. Their father said I had to remain outside until dinner was over. I'm sure he wondered why I wasn't home having dinner with my family. Then again, maybe he knew.

I'd wait patiently for Kabeena and Brenda to come outside and play, clasping hold of my shaky knees, trying to control my breathing. I knew a game of hide and seek or kick the can would ease my trembling body.

The games would end when the street lights came on and we had to go home. Perhaps I had missed supper. I didn't care. Slowly pushing open the front door, my ears on high alert, I would test the air, listening for silence. Was the house quiet? If so, I slipped back in. Elaine and Dick in their rooms doing homework and the hum of Momma's Singer sewing machine meant the coast was clear. Dad was slurping down coffee at the kitchen table, a thin smokey halo shrouding his head. I would rush past with nary a glance. Maybe he mumbled something, but if it wasn't in a tolerable tone, I didn't respond.

When nights of shouting became unbearable, I'd jump into bed and pull the covers over my head. The warmth of the blanket made a snug tent. My cocoon of sheets kept me oblivious to the world outside my door. It was my secret hiding place. My bedroom was next to the kitchen. The blanket muffled the raging voices from the other side of that closed door.

"Hey, God," I'd say. "It's me again. I'm hiding. No one knows I'm here." It was like when a small child stands in front of you, covers their eyes, and thinks they're unseen. That was me. I wanted God to hear me. I created an undercover fantasy family with a father that worked, and a mother who spent days baking chocolate cake with banana filling smothered in rich, creamy chocolate frosting.

15

I felt the presence of God. The peacefulness erased my surroundings. With my favorite toy dog clutched in my arms, I fell asleep.

In the morning, sunlight seeped through the thin brown blanket, removing my protective walls. The safety net disappeared, thrusting me out from under and into the new day. Who knows? Maybe today would be a better day. I could always hope.

Did I wonder if other kids lived like this? Maybe. I knew my friends' fathers weren't like ours. My cousins' fathers weren't like ours, either. Did I wish Dad would just vanish one day? Maybe. But wishing our lives were different just made me sad. Our lives were like an annoying wart that we hoped would heal soon. We were learning early that life has no guarantees. It was now filled with unplanned chaos. We put one foot in front of the other and shuffled forward.

Chapter 4

You Get What You Get
and You Don't Throw a Fit

There was no money coming in. How frightening this must have been for Momma. Dad couldn't hold down a job, that was certain, and she wasn't working. Would we now live in penury for the rest of our lives? Perhaps her brothers helped out with money for food. One time, our uncle, who lived on a farm, gave her a box of meat. Our ice box wasn't very large, and Momma placed the newspaper-wrapped meat outside the back door. Unfortunately, it was near the garbage cans. Garbage men, at that time, entered your yard, picked up the garbage cans, took them to the street and dumped them into the garbage truck. They must have mistaken her box of meat for garbage. Frantically, half crazed out of her mind, Momma called city hall's sanitation department, to no avail. No one had a clue as to where her box of meat had gone. I'm guessing it was Campbell's soup every day for a week.

In Milwaukee, everyone went "by Schuster's." There was a favorite saying: "I'll meet you by Schuster's where the streetcar goes 'round the bend." Another saying was: "Where are you going? I'm going by Schuster's, by George."

Schuster's department store was a three-story building at 12th and Vilet. You wondered if anyone ever went into Schuster's. Well, my mother did, because she was hired to sell hats there. She started out part time, but after a few years became a full-time employee. Two years of attending teachers' college before her marriage had prepared her to teach in a one-room schoolhouse in Port Washington, but marrying Dad had erased that option. She would now have to rein-vent herself—teaching in a one-room schoolhouse was not possible; in those days, you could not be married and teach.

With Momma working, I guess Dad was now the "stay at home" parent looking after us. I don't think he hung around much. When I asked a cousin in Chicago, who had stayed with us a lot, what he re-membered about my father, he said, "I thought, well, that's cool, your mother works and your dad stays home." Kids do not complicate life with in-depth thinking.

My sister Elaine, three years older than I, was the boss. My brother Dick is a year younger than I, so we both did pretty much what Elaine ordered us to do. For lunchtime, Momma would leave us a can of chicken noodle soup. Elaine warmed it up, set three bowls on the kitchen table, and ladled it out. Dick and I, noses table high, eyes never wavering, watched as she divided the soup into the bowls. We were making sure there was a fair number of noodles in each bowl. Luckily for us, we liked soda crackers slathered with butter, washed down with glass after glass of Kool-Aid.

Other days we made veggie sandwiches. We buttered two slices of white bread, then layered the bread with slices of green onions, rad-ishes, and cucumbers. We were ahead of our time with these creations.

In today's world, Momma would have been jailed for leaving us pretty much by ourselves, because, let's face it, Dad was not home all the time. Being by ourselves made us independent. We were masters of inventing creative play; an imagination was all you needed. There were no play dates or planned activities. We were free range kids.

In autumn, we raked fallen leaves into piles, then divided the piles. We used the leaves to delineate rooms on the front lawn. We created stories about who lived in those leaf homes.

We repurposed an old kitchen sink into a turtle's wonderland. One side had sand with a small board ladder leading to the other side, which was filled with water. Turtles were 39 cents at Woolworths. They didn't seem to last long. We held elaborate funerals in the garden with popsicle-stick markers and bleeding-heart flowers.

In winter, when the snow was deep, we dug snow forts and climbed inside, safe from snowball fights.

We spent many hours outside. Nature was our outdoor home.

The empty field behind our house had a huge indentation in the ground where we kids could sit and set plans into action. Sky-high trees provided shade and cover like a secret hideout. We only allowed a few other kids from our street to share this field with us. It was *our* field, our play station. Our father never bothered us there.

Games of Monopoly, Parcheesi, and Authors kept us from squabbling on rainy days.

If it was a rainy day, Elaine, Dick, and I spent hours in the attic. We loved that stuffy, dust-filled place. When you consider dust is composed of 50 percent dead skin cells, perhaps our ancestors were guiding us. The light filtering through the windows showcased the sparkling dust motes floating in the air. The room was spacious, and the high ceiling kept it somewhat cool in summer. Looking out the third-story windows, we felt hidden. We were safe, tucked into Rapunzel's tower, undisturbed in our special place. No one was permitted there but us. Dick and I painted the soot-covered floor to make trails for Dick's American Flyer train tracks. His huge train engine puffed and smelled like a real train while pulling two Pullman cars, a coal car, a flatbed and, of course, a red caboose. I loved stuffing my dolls into the Pullman cars as Dick ran the controls. Momma provided paint, and we covered a large floor area with our artistic creations.

Many forgotten treasures were stored in the attic—items overlooked or abandoned by various tenants and relatives from long ago. There should be an attic in every house, a place to store parts of folks' life stories waiting to be discovered by future generations. Every so often we'd open Great-Grandma's gigantic steamer trunks, wondering what treasures she had brought from Germany. Were there dried tear drops staining the rose-covered interior lining? How many times had those trunks crossed the ocean? Huge white funeral baskets stood under the eave. Whose funeral? We didn't know.

When we pulled open the large closet door, the pungent cedar smell cleaned our nostrils. Our winter coats were stored there, safe from marauding moths. There was a Civil War sword on the wall near an old deer head, and once in a while we snuck a glance at the old human skull in the shadows. No one knows who hung it there.

Elaine would curl up on the dusty window seat reading and re-reading her favorite book, *Baby Island*, by Carol Ryrie Brink. It was a type of Robinson Crusoe tale but with female heroines. A neighbor, living on the street behind our house, fostered twin baby girls. Elaine would spend hours playing with them and asked Momma if she would adopt them or trade them for me. I guess Momma already had enough mouths to feed; she just laughed. I didn't share her humor and kept an eagle eye on my sister.

The attic holds a special place in my heart. Play there was uninhibited, and memories were retained for safekeeping. We could pretend our life was more like one found in the pages of a favorite book.

Tante Anna, one of Dad's sisters, stepped in on many a summer day. Like a fairy godmother, she weaved her zest for life into our sparse existence, creating a fissure for an unknown wonderland to seep in. She insisted we call her Tante and not Aunt, and we obliged her. When something went wrong, she would cheer us up with, "Now you have a story to tell." Tante Anna was truly a *sui generis* person.

The day Tante Anna took us to Schuster's for their famous hot fudge sundae with mint ice cream, we strolled past the hat bar where Momma worked. I stopped in my tracks. Momma looked like a schoolgirl, almost unrecognizable! Her youthful face, her eyes brimming with merriment; none of her home life showed.

"What a pretty woman," Elaine said, beaming. "And she is our mother!"

Momma's dark brown, white-polka-dotted, belted dress showed

off her youthful body. Her short, dark hair flipped around her face. She and her co-worker were gaily tossing a hat back and forth. Rays of happiness shone from her smiling face. I felt a sudden giddiness as I watched her tomfoolery. That erased some of the guilt I felt for the hot fudge sundaes we were about to indulge in while she was working.

Department store wages couldn't support a family of five, so at night we heard Momma practicing on her old Royal typewriter. Allstate Insurance hired her in the accounting department. There she remained a faithful employee for 27 years, way past retirement age.

"I loved figures," she said later. "In school I took every math course—algebra, geometry, calculus. It was a perfect fit for me."

A supervisor apologized for not being able to pay her the same wage as the men doing similar work. She had hit the glass ceiling, even though she was the sole support of five folks. The facts didn't bother her; she kept giving 110% anyway. She was so accepting. Or was she just grateful that the job provided security for her family?

Chapter 5

Enduring Shadow Life

Milwaukee was a good place to grow up in the 1940s and '50s. The acres of uninterrupted emerald lawns and huge maple trees were a pleasure to live among. In autumn, the transformation of the maple trees popped a brilliant orange or shimmering gold or bright sunflower-yellow that grabbed your attention.

In summer, the city parks, with their towering pine trees and rolling hills, were filled with frolicking kids flying kites and playing pick-up baseball games or croquet, and old men squabbling over a bocce ball. Here and there young lovers huddled discreetly on a Packers blanket. Gray-bearded men drank beer, reliving past lives in countries left behind. The smell of brats on the grill filled the air—brats made the Wisconsin way, marinated in beer. Picnic areas were claimed early, their tables laden with overflowing picnic baskets. The Europeans who had settled Milwaukee loved nature, and their parks reflected remembrances of beloved countries.

In the 1920s, one could ride the streetcar downtown to many festive beer gardens. As you stepped off the streetcar, the jolly sounds of an oom-pah band had your toes tapping and made you eager to whirl around the dance floor. Polkas, the Schottische … no one wanted to miss out. Good German beer was guzzled, steins were raised in toasts, German drinking songs were belted out. Brats, and probably a Polish wurst or two, were eaten. Sundays were filled with music, laughter, and friends. At one time Milwaukee held the title "The Deutsche Athens of the Midwest."

Later the beer gardens disappeared, but not the picnics in the park. Wisconsin folks loved to socialize, and the city parks were a reflection of this. The parks were the spot for family gatherings in summer, and many churches planned annual events there.

Each year our church held its summer event in Washington Park. Women covered wooden picnic tables with white paper cloths, then set out dishes of macaroni salad, slumgullion, egg salad, warm German potato salad, Wisconsin cheddar cheese slices, Milwaukee rye bread (the kind with salt on the crust), cheese curds, kosher dill pickles, sponge cakes, chocolate cupcakes, lemon pies, apple pies, peach kuchens—the tables seemed to sag under the weight of it all.

It was the hot dogs we kids went for. Toasted on the grill, smothered in ketchup, mustard, and relish; you could eat as many as you liked. No one counted how many boxes of Cracker Jack you took, either. Trouble with Cracker Jack, you had to eat the entire box because the prize you craved waited at the bottom. Some cheap plastic coveted toy was yours to keep. Dixie cups, chocolate or vanilla with tiny wooden spoons attached to the top, paddle pops, and as much soda as your tiny stomach could hold was all for the taking. Grownups looked the other way.

Games were set up with luxurious prizes for the winners. Miss James, an employee at the Milwaukee Recreation Department, ruled the games. There were races: donkey races, three-legged races, relays, you name it. There was tug-of-war for the adults and a race tying husband and wife together, hopping to the finish line.

One thing diminished the picnic's joy for us: Momma standing on the sidelines in her beige pedal pushers and crisp sleeveless white blouse, all alone. She seemed resigned to her role of' "husbandless woman," and she stood with determination and grit.

"Penny search is about to happen!" some man would belt out. "Kids, come gather over here!" That got us running. A large sheet of canvas was placed on the ground; bag after bag of sawdust was dumped in the middle, piled high. "Back, all you kids!" the men would yell as they opened rolls and rolls of pennies. Yes, pennies!

The pennies were dumped into the middle of the sawdust pile. We kids would hold onto each other's arms, making sure no one slipped in ahead of the whistle. Panting heavily, eyes glued on the prize, we anxiously awaited the signal. When Miss James blew her red whistle, mayhem ensued. Everyone rushed to jump into the sawdust. Sawdust coated our hot, sweaty arms, our legs, our hair. We didn't care; we were going to get MONEY. "You can keep all you find," someone would shout. Well, small hands had a hard time holding onto pennies. Lucky for us some pennies stuck to our sweaty hands. You dropped more than you held. If you were lucky, you came out with a total of ten cents and a huge smile on your face.

I had always wanted a dog. Kittens had followed me home from school, but they never hung around long. I plastered telephone poles with "Missing Kitten" posters, but no one ever returned them. While I was knee deep in sawdust, I felt a wet nose on my leg. God, I hoped it wasn't Randolph with his perpetual snotty nose! It was not. It was a frisky little black terrier with four white paws, a white star on his chest, and two bushy brown eyebrows, nosing the sawdust and wondering what all the fuss was about.

A shout of "Dog!" went up, and many of us chased after the rascally canine. It ran to an elderly man hunched over on a park bench, who grabbed hold of its collar and said to all of us, "Do any of you want a dog? I'm moving into a retirement home and I can't keep a dog. He's yours, whoever wants him. His name is Rex." His voice sounded sad.

Dick and I rushed to find our mother. "Momma, Mom," we screamed. "There's this really old man and he said we can have his dog. Can we? Can we, please?"

She laughed and said, "Yes, if no one else wants him." Either the drink in her hand wasn't soda, or she didn't believe this would happen. She said yes!

Dick and I made a mad dash back to the old man, only to discover that some other little fella had beat us to the dog. "My mom said I could keep him," he said smugly, grabbing hold of the leash.

Slowly we made our way back to the picnic and told Momma what had happened. To cheer us up she said, "Well, if he can't keep him, we can have him." I think back, what a woman! The fact that she would introduce a dog into our dysfunctional lives still leaves me in awe.

That evening, our doorbell rang. There stood the little boy with the dog, Rex. "I can't keep him," he said sadly, handing over the leash. Rex bounded in the door, and we took off his leash. French doors separated our front room from the hallway. Rex stopped by the doors, peed on the floor-length lace curtains, then tore past the piano into the bedroom where Momma was sewing, scattering her patterns on the floor. As she scooped them up, Rex ran into the kitchen and back to the front room. He was now our dog.

After Rex made his exploratory rounds, he stood in front of us, one ear cocked, both brown eyebrows raised, head to the side, looking us in the eye as if to say, "I know, I know, you need me." He seemed to intuit our need for his love. If you reverse the spelling of dog… well, it makes you wonder.

Rex was never confined to the basement but settled himself into the pink chair in the back room and considered himself part of this family—or chairman of the board! He was a mutt, a mixture of many breeds, mostly terrier. His tail was like a baton, long and skinny. One of our farm uncles said, upon seeing Rex, "Cut that damn tail off, it's too long." We never left him alone with Rex after that remark.

Rex especially seemed to perceive our father's needs. The two of them were inseparable. At lunchtime, Rex got a share of Dad's sandwiches. He provided a love and understanding that my father needed. Wherever Dad went during the day, the dog was with him. He never put Rex on a leash, but he made us use a leash.

Let me tell you about the leash. Dad went down the basement and cut ten feet off of Momma's washline. He tied it to Rex's collar, and Dick or I held onto the other end. "A dog needs freedom," Dad said. On our walks, there were times when Rex was on one side of the street while we were still on the other, waiting to cross, the long leash holding up traffic in the middle.

Rex was Dad's faithful companion, but he also had his own agenda. He had a purpose in life. When I think about Rex now, he reminds me of the dogs in Peru who congregate daily on the boulevards of the main streets, just lounging around, socializing. At dusk, all the dogs return to their homes to guard and protect their owners.

Rex could be considered a lothario about town. Some nights, when he smelled a female in heat (up to five miles away!), he'd howl, "Hang on, I'm coming." Momma would get up and let him out, muttering, "Get out of here, you dang mutt." Rex would be gone all night; the next morning, he'd slink home, stinking and tired, then sleep the day away.

We had the service of a doctor, who lived three blocks down. "Take this payment to the doctor," Momma instructed. Rex and I walked a few blocks to the doctor's house. The doctor's wife looked annoyed when she opened the door. "Is this your dog?" she snapped.

"Why, yes," I said. "Do you know him?"

"We have a litter of puppies in the backyard from him," she replied angrily.

I think the bill doubled.

Mr. Fitzpatrick, our elderly neighbor, was kneeling in the chapel at Holy Cross Church, nine blocks away. He looked down; there sat Rex, patiently waiting. Reaching down, he scratched Rex's ears, and together they strolled back home.

Rex commandeered the pink chair in the back room. If you mistakenly sat in his chair, he placed his paw on your leg and moaned. Drool escaped, a wet nose caressed your leg, and a look in his eye said, "You know this is my chair." So of course we would move to another location. Rex would settle in and look around, as if to say, "Now, isn't life grand?" until he silently tooted, sending us scrambling for the door.

As much as Rex loved Dad, if he heard the back door rattling off its hinges … that deep, surly, voice … the snarly "Where's that damn dog," Rex swiftly disappeared. I never knew where he hid, but he wouldn't come out until morning. Although Rex was love, his love was not given lightly. Come morning, if all was well, he would give Dad another chance.

Looking back, I'm amazed at Momma's tolerance in allowing this independent animal, who often had to be bailed out of the dog pound, into our mishmash household. Sometimes Rex ran away if he hadn't been quick enough to hide when Dad was on a rampage. Rex wouldn't stay by his side until Dad was sober.

Our car was gone by then, so it wasn't possible for Dad to drive, and Momma never learned how. One time, when Rex ran away from Dad, we called Momma at work and asked her if we could take a taxi to the dog pound. "Oh, no," she said. "Don't do that." So, we had to beg a neighbor to fetch our dog from the pound. In later years, it was my sister's boyfriend who had to free Rex from the pound. He still stuck around; I can't say he wasn't in on the secret.

Rex stayed around for many years, providing comfort during those turbulent times. The wet nose, something soft to cling to, the knowing look on his face—a perfect imperfect dog for an imperfect family. His tolerance and forgiveness filled our aching bodies with so much needed love. In later life, when I'd see a black terrier with four white paws, a white star on his chest, and two bushy brown eyebrows, I would think, "I bet I knew your father."

Chapter 6

Books, the Gateway to Oz

The laziness of a hot, humid day was perfect for roller skating down the sidewalk with pigtails flying in the breeze, scraped knees, and pitchers of Kool-Aid. In and out of the house we went, gulping down cool glasses of the sweet punch: a large red-and-yellow-striped pitcher filled to the top with cold water to which a packet of orange, raspberry, lime or cherry Kool-Aid and a cup of sugar had been added.

We made popsicles using ice cube trays with toothpicks for handles. While maneuvering the trays to the icebox, liquid almost always spilled on the floor. Come Saturday, cleaning day, one of us would be down on our hands and knees scrubbing the floors or the back stairs. Momma hated dirty floors and stairs. It was either that or hang the laundry on the zig-zag wash lines across the backyard. (Actually, I loved hanging the laundry outside. I don't know why, but I did. Maybe in another lifetime I was a happy washerwoman in a sane home.) Bright white sheets and pillowcases were hung on the wash line seen from Wisconsin Avenue. Underwear was discreetly hidden on an inside wash line. The last line held the pants and socks, which I always hung in pairs thinking they liked to talk to each other. When I was very young, my mother strung a small wash line between two posts so I could wash my doll's clothes. Come Sunday, all wash lines were bare.

We didn't need alarm clocks to wake us up on summer mornings. The katydids and yakking blue jays did that job, forecasting the coming day's temperature. Tucking our pajamas under our pillows, we'd scramble into plaid shorts, sandals, and cool cotton shirts. Hurrying to answer the doorbell, we'd find Brenda and Kabeena waiting patiently on the porch. "Hey, want to walk to the library? We finished all our books."

The five of us would walk to the neighborhood library at 35th and Clybourne, twelve blocks away. Frank Zeidler, our cousin and mayor of Milwaukee, had been instrumental in securing neighborhood libraries.

Sometimes Elaine, Dick, and I would walk by ourselves, chattering away as we stepped over the cracks in the sidewalk. We'd cross 47th Street and glance at the tall standing billboards, so inviting to climb on. Once Dick and I climbed up the back of one of those billboards. We were so excited to reach the top, until Dick upset a wasp nest. Screaming hysterically, we rushed home to remedy his pain.

Sometimes we'd stop at Ace Foods, peering into the windows, watching the frozen custard cascading out of the machine. Penniless, licking our chops, we wished we could buy a cone brimming with that creamy custard.

The viaduct loomed in front of us. Our hearts beat faster, our legs broke into a run. The long concrete bridge was always windy, and the loud whoosh of passing cars added to the excitement of crossing it. The viaduct had won an award in 1911 for its Art Deco design. Large vaulted arches hung from the sides of this structure, which crossed the Menomonee River. We'd stop to peer over the steep side, holding on to each other as we'd take a look at the Miller High Life brewery on the left and Piggsville on the right. The viaduct was almost a mile long.

With our feet rushing now to escape the wind and automobile noise, we'd reach the stairs, which came out halfway along the viaduct. "Oh, it smells like pee!" we'd cry, holding our noses. "Someone must have peed on these steps," I said.

After World War II, hobos lived under the viaduct. No money, no jobs, nowhere to go. Once a hobo, shabbily dressed, knocked on our front door asking for food. Momma made him a huge bologna sandwich and gave him a cup of coffee. I hid behind her, arms around her waist, peeking out at this scruffy, unidentified man as she made small talk with him. When he finished the coffee, he thanked her. She smiled and waited until he was gone, then she threw the cup away.

Piggsville, named by a former pig farmer, was quiet. Two-story frame-structured Milwaukee bungalows graced the streets. Many Eastern Europeans lived here and worked at the Miller brewery. Through the village we hiked, up the hill to our beloved two-story, cream-colored neighborhood library, where I had gotten my first library card.

We quenched our thirst with a drink from the bubbler before pushing open the heavy library door. Entering the building, we scattered in all directions. We ransacked the shelves, seeking the land of fantasy and imagination. Sitting on the wooden floor surrounded by my favorite books, I could have remained in this haven forever, pulling out Nancy Drew mysteries and Sue Barton nurse books. (I wonder why I liked nurse books, when even a splinter in my foot made me shudder?)

Time was nonexistent in the library. I lived among the pages, unaware of my surroundings, hungry to explore unknown places. I was consumed by one tale after another, knowing each page would send me to undiscovered lifestyles, people whose families didn't reflect mine. The stories of people traveling by car or train increased my curiosity. I could picture myself sleeping on the high bed of the train and eating chocolate ice cream from silver dishes on white linen-covered tables. Someday, I told myself, I would take a train ride and travel the world. When the others, books in hand, were ready to leave, I dragged myself to the checkout counter, handed over my precious library card, and took possession of my five-book limit.

Walking back the way we came, we encountered a strange man. He wanted us to come home with him. We knew about not talking to strangers, even then. "No way," we yelled, taking off down the sidewalk. But not before he bopped each of us on the head with his loaf of Wonder Bread.

The cool porch awaited us. Plopping our tushes onto the purple glider swing, we delved into our new books. The Moffat Family series showcased life situations I savored. Elaine eagerly turned the pages of *Mrs. Mike* or a Nancy Drew mystery. The Nancy Drew books were so scary Elaine only read them in the safety of the glider gathering. Time rolled on as we sucked on our homemade popsicles, deep in stories. It was peaceful.

Sometimes my father wasn't home when we returned. He was in and out all day—who knows where he went. He had the propensity to walk aimlessly up and down Wisconsin Avenue or Wells Street onto Bluemound Road, lost in a world of his own. I often wondered if he ever sat down, or if he just ambled on and on. Did he scare folks off with his incoherent mumbling, his unfocused eyes? His life seemed to contain an overwhelming amount of ennui.

Knowing he was not home, we let our guard down, relaxing in the quiet peacefulness, the sanity of it all. Rex came out and snuggled by our feet, panting in the heat. Some summer days were like a dream, but we never trusted those feelings. We just savored the sweet, languid moments.

Chapter 7

Imagination is Our Salvation

Summer vacation. Momma was working full time at Allstate Insurance, and Tante Anna knew we were home alone. Tante Anna preferred company to housework. She told stories of when she, my father, and their other siblings were young, how their house was a constant stream of friends and relatives popping in.

There was always the alluring smell of roasted coffee beans drawing folks into their warm kitchen. Fresh-out-of-the-oven cinnamon coffee cake cooled on the table; German cheesecake and crullers on a flowered china plate welcomed one to sit and coffee klatch. Many relatives lived in close proximity and visited daily. Children weren't doted on. Conversations were for adults, and children created their own excitement outdoors.

Dad and Tante Anna grew up in the house we were now living in—a house over a hundred years old. Three generations had lived here. It stood three stories high on what was then called Grand Avenue but was changed to Wisconsin Avenue in the late 1940s. It had been part of the town of Wauwatosa before it was annexed into Milwaukee. Dad jokingly referred to his boyhood home as the Hotel De Gink. Tante Anna called it the Clubhouse. To me, it was the German Compound.

Some mornings we were awakened by the telephone ringing. "Elaine, Kathleen, and Dicky!" The authoritative voice of Tante Anna shook the lethargy from our sleepy bodies. "I need you to come and help me move some boxes," she said, then abruptly hung up her phone. The morning heat made us want to linger in bed a little longer.

"Shake a leg," my sister directed, and we did. Bounding out the door, skipping breakfast, marching in a line, schlepping past the Salvage's brown brick house with their polio-stricken daughter and garage full of stashed cash (that's what their son told us!). God, I wanted so much to take a peek in there!

We passed the one-story white stucco house with the wide veranda and green trim where Kabeena and Brenda lived. They were in Canada on vacation. I wondered what Canada looked like. The farthest away I had ever been was Chicago, where our Italian uncle and his family lived. Visiting his fish house was a succulent delight. Just picturing those plump, juicy smoked fish made my empty stomach growl. Inside his fish house he'd flip baskets of shrimp into his special breading, hot fryers waiting to finish the process. Those spicy French-fried shrimp never needed sauce. Flavor exploded with each crunch. We never left there without a bag of shrimp fresh from the fryer. Photographs of Lena Horne graced the fish house walls.

The first kidnapping we ever heard of happened while we were staying with our Chicago relatives, who lived in an apartment building on Addison Avenue. Someone climbed through a window and took a child. Hearing that news awakened a new fear. I felt the world was leaving us unprotected. It was like Dorothy realizing she wasn't in Kansas anymore. Danger lurked everywhere. Elaine and I shared an upstairs bedroom at that time. She told me to sleep near the window; that way, when the kidnapper came in, he'd get me first. I kept the window closed.

As we trudged along to Tante Anna's house, we passed Hawley Road School. The elementary school was closed for summer vacation. Miss Gay was my kindergarten teacher there; her memory is forever printed on my heart. When I graduated from high school, she sent me a congratulations card. I wonder if she compiled a scrapbook of all her students. Her ability to pull a student into the world of knowledge made school a joyful experience for me.

At school, being drawn from my embryonic state into unfathomable awareness was exciting. It was a new awakening. (A note in my baby book comments, "Kathleen has quit misbehaving now she has entered school." Maybe it should have said, "Now that she is able to read"). Sitting in the Bluebird Circle, reading my very first book, created an insatiable appetite for words. I remember the thrill of opening a book and devouring its contents, words on the page revealing the wonderment of the unknown.

"Words!" a visitor once told us in sixth grade "Learn words, words, and more words!" I was too shy to speak up and inquire what he meant by "more words."

My love of books began in the Bluebird Circle and continues to this day. I'm never without a book.

Everyone on my father's side of the family had attended Hawley Road School: Dad, his siblings, and all my Geuder cousins. You'd think there would be a Geuder plaque hung by the school office, as I'm sure we all had frequented that room when summoned to the principal's office. Some secrets shouldn't be revealed.

Sixtieth Street was zooming with cars, demanding our attention. As we crossed the street we entered Wauwatosa. Tante Anna's small bungalow sat back on a hill. Its white siding, gray roof, attached sun porch, and crisp white lace curtains blowing out the front windows reminded me of a charming dollhouse oozing with cheerfulness. To take part in that cheer, all you had to do was enter the front door.

"We're here!" we announced, walking right in. Tante Anna, as always, stood with cigarette in hand, glasses pushed back on her small nose, short brown hair neat and trim. She was wearing a green flowered house dress (she never wore pants), comfortable brown shoes, and a broad smile. We were always welcome here. "Come on, get in here," she boomed in her loud voice. We could hear the Heinie and His Grenadiers polka band playing on the radio in the kitchen. Their music, quite popular in Milwaukee, was a noontime ritual for Tante Anna. I'll bet she was a little wild in her youth. Did she polka around the kitchen when no one was looking?

35

"Okay," she said, "let's get busy. We've got work to do downstairs." We weren't in a big rush as we weren't too sure of how BIG a project awaited us.

There were three big boxes we had to move from the laundry room to the recreation room. We each took hold of one side of a box and heave ho, away we went.

"Stack them over by the jukebox," Tante Anna said.

My fingers were itching to push a few buttons and play a song, but there was no time today. I remember the parties these adults had. They knew how to celebrate. Kids were never allowed to join. They deposited the kids on the upstairs bed, covered with discarded coats. It was impossible to sleep amidst all their laughing, shouting, stomping feet downstairs. Once I slipped down the stairs to take a look. Along with Momma and Dad, several of my aunts and uncles were dancing up a storm. They were doing the Virginia Reel. Auntie, prim and proper Auntie, had on someone's union suit; the trap door hung open displaying her shiny behind. Her do-si-do partner, Uncle Ervin, had on a similar suit, his open trap door baring his pink behind. They do-si-doed up and down the line and back again. A difficult sight to erase from your memory. Fun existed with or without funds.

"That's enough work for today," Tante Anna said.

Breathing a sigh of relief, we visited Tante's player piano. I wanted to feed it a music roll and watch the keys bounce up and down. I wanted to place my fingers on the keys and pretend I was playing like my father. But it would have to wait for another time.

"I need to fetch my chicken feed," Tante Anna smiled, plunking her going-out hat on her head and starting up the stairs.

We knew what that meant! We were heading to Gilles Frozen Custard for lunch. Dick and I shoved each other trying to get up the stairs first. Everyone went to Gilles. They had the best frozen custard in Milwaukee. Weddings were held there, high school kids congregated after school there. Bud Selig, a Jewish kid from Milwaukee, now the Commissioner of Baseball, ate there every day, and we were going to eat there, too. We'd have a hot dog, a Coke, and a big hot fudge sundae with pecans. The custard was creamy and fresh—no cheap ingredients, just rich Wisconsin milk with fresh dairy cream, sugar, and farm eggs. The hot fudge was smooth, and the pecans were fresh and salty. Spoiled by Gilles, we were always disappointed to experience stale pecans at other restaurants. Interesting note: Tante Anna's husband, our Uncle Walter, was asked to invest in Gilles when they first opened, but he didn't think it would be successful. He may have thought different if he'd known that Tante Anna would become their number-one customer!

Uncle Walter owned a mechanic's garage where he employed my father part time, pumping gas. The job made Dad feel useful, but the pay contributed to his beer money.

We stopped at the garage before we went to Gilles. It was noon, and Tante Anna packed her husband's daily lunch in a green wicker basket. There would be a hot dish, some fruit, a cookie, and a large thermos of coffee, all covered with a red-checked cloth.

Leaning in the car window, Uncle Walter loved to tease, "I suppose you're all going to Gilles and I have to eat this lunch."

"Yes!" I sang out, "And you can't come with us!" I stuck my tongue out at him and whipped my pigtails back inside the window before he could grab hold of them.

No one brought Dad any lunch. I saw him slouched over, legs crossed, puffing on a cigarette, sitting in the office chair waiting for someone to need gas. His sad eyes and slight smile made my stomach ache. His forlorn face erased some of my excitement. He had on his orange sweater buttoned up tightly. I waved to him, and he gave me a small smile—so lonely looking. I wondered who he was listening to in his head. Did his fellow garage workers engage him in conversation? Or did they just work around him, like he was an invisible person?

What were his thoughts other than the constant refrain, "I'm taking up room. I just need a pine box"? Maybe the realization that he wasn't contributing much to life? Why didn't he try to change his behavior? I still thought he was just an alcoholic and capable of changing his behavior on his own.

After filling our stomachs with pure delight at Gilles, we headed to our next favorite spot, the Village. Wauwatosa had a romantic riverside village look, complete with daily trains and picturesque train stations. The shops were set in quaint brown-brick buildings, and soon we'd be inside the dime store. Elaine and I rushed to where the paper doll booklets were displayed. Some folks called them paper dolls, but to me they were treasured cut-outs. They provided me with an escape hatch, whisking me off into the land of imagination. My sister and I chose the cut-out book called "Star Babies." In later life I discovered these paper dolls were created by a famous German artist. Their faces are reminiscent of Hummel's creations. Dick usually got a model airplane or a squirt gun or an Archie comic book. But the fun didn't end there.

"Wait!" Tante Anna would stop us as we were clambering out of the car. "I need one of you to empty the chicken feed for me."

That pleasant chore fell to the kid sitting closest to her. Chicken feed was the change at the bottom of her purse. She threw all her change into her purse, and the accumulation made it too heavy to carry. Once it was emptied, we divided the pennies, nickels, and dimes among the three of us, dutifully thanked Tante Anna, and rushed indoors to play.

Now my treasured paper dolls would be carefully cut out and arranged into families. The fantasy families I created made my home life disappear. I would spread them over the couch cushions, living now within my stories.

Once, when Dad came crashing home, knocking kitchen chairs onto the floor, his snarling words bouncing off the walls, his face boiling with pent-up rage, I hurriedly packed up my cut-outs, throwing them in a box. Out the door I fled and up the street I ran to Tante Anna's house. Never asking why I was there with a box of paper dolls under my arm and tears running down my cheeks, she let me in. I quickly went to her living room, unpacked my cut-outs, put my happy families back together on her cushions, and resumed my stories. I played until I had to drag myself back down the block and home again.

Sometimes the sun shone through those gloomy days with a glimpse of a rainbow. Sometimes!

Chapter 8

Thanksgiving Gathering

Mmmmm … whiffs of succulent turkey snuck in and around my nose, waking me from a deep slumber. My bare feet hit the cold floor as I bounded out of bed. I searched hurriedly for some warm woolen socks. On below-zero days, I would haul my clothes under the covers and dress there. Today, though, I quickly pulled on my green woolen sweater to capture the heat left over from sleep. It was a special day. I would wear the yellow jumper that Momma had made, the one with blue flowers embroidered on the bib. Elaine had a matching blue jumper with yellow daisies on her bib. We'd look like the Bobbsey Twins.

I bounded down the back stairs in my brand new Buster Brown black patent-leather Mary Janes, clickety-clacking on the wooden stairs. Excitement was building in my mind. My stomach growling, I hurried up the short steps from the back hall into the kitchen. The inviting smells beckoned me into the warm kitchen, where a turkey had been roasting in the oven since dawn. Dinner preparations were well underway.

Luscious lemon pie filling was simmering on the stove, and Momma was whipping egg white to stiff peaks. I stuck my finger in the warm pie filling and ran for my life. Would there be time to make potato dumplings, I wondered? They were time consuming. Momma made a dough with mashed potatoes, a little flour, and some eggs, squeezed it into balls, and threw the dumplings into boiling water for ten minutes or so. I should have paid closer attention to how to make them; I'd sure like to make some now.

Breakfast was slim, all energies poured into the great feast. Dick and I pushed each other, trying to be the chosen one to grind the fresh cranberries. It was fun to fill the grinder with cranberries, crank the handle, and watch the squished berry pulp plop out in globs.

"Pour the berries in slowly," Momma reminded Dick, who beat me to the grinder. The metal grinder was attached to the cutting board on the counter. A bowl was set on the floor under the grinder to catch the blood-red cranberry juice. Momma would hand me s sliced orange, me being the designated orange-slice dropper. In between handfuls of cranberries, I dropped the orange slices, rind and all, into the grinder. Momma added sugar, finishing the cranberry relish.

The potatoes were boiled and removed from the stove. Momma, with her strong farm-girl arms, whipped towering mounds of mashed potatoes that, come dinner time, would be smothered in her never-lumpy, satiny turkey gravy. I never did learn how to make gravy without lumps. Another missed opportunity.

Dad was in a relatively good mood. Maybe the comforting smell of turkey soothed his turbulent mind. He pulled the dining room table out from under the front window. With two leaves inserted, the table extended past the piano and into the hallway. We assisted in bringing out the table mats that cushioned the good china. Carefully we laid the lace tablecloth over the mats. The cloth was once used in another time, another country, a time when they too gathered around it for happy conversations, good food, and laughter. It was sent to us in exchange for flour, sugar, coffee, stockings, and tea. The cloth held many memories, and now our stories were being added.

Soon our rooms would be filled with cigar smoke, loud voices, laughter, and plenty of jokes. Tiny, elfin Uncle Eddie arrived first. His bald head was as shiny as his huge smile. His mischievous eyes brimmed with laughter as he spilled joke after joke, laughing as hard as we did.

Blind Uncle Joe and Aunt Ida were next to arrive. Uncle Joe's voice was loud. "Olga, that dinner smells delicious!" he shouted out to Momma. Aunt Ida, always laughing, excited to be here, clamored on and on. Joe and Ida didn't have any children, so they looked forward to being part of Momma's party.

Last to arrive were stately, conservative Uncle John and his very proper wife, Auntie. Her name was really Hildegarde, but on a Sunday visit to our grandmother's farm, we kids decided it took too long to say her name. I was designated by my older sister to give Aunt Hildegarde the news. "Aunt Hildegarde," I sucked in my breath. "We have decided your name takes too long to say and from now on we're going to call you Auntie." She was sitting in the front seat of the car. With her neck stiff and erect and her nose tilted to the sky, she slowly turned and eyed me coolly, one eyebrow cocked, hesitating for effect. "Okay," she whispered. And from then on, she was Auntie.

Auntie and Uncle John were childless, so they took us under their wing. A beauty-salon owner, Auntie determined when Elaine's and my hair needed cutting. Short-short is what she liked. We hated to see her hop out of the car with her dreaded shears. Elaine went first while I waited smugly outside. Out came Elaine, bawling her head off, her sweater pulled over her head, sobbing by the tree. I made the mistake of laughing. "Wait till it's your turn," she screamed at me. It wasn't long after that I came out, a sweater pulled over my head, bawling on the other side of the tree.

A bona fide customer of Auntie's was the celebrity Milwaukee saloon owner "Dirty Helen." Dirty Helen's bar had no chairs; customers had to stand. The bar was stocked with two bottles of brandy. When the bottles were empty, she called a cab to fetch her two more bottles. It was a big hit with tourists. Dirty Helen's weekly appointment with Auntie was on Sunday after church. We had to remain in Uncle John's car, patiently waiting for Auntie to finish her appointment and exit the saloon. Never did we get to meet the infamous Dirty Helen.

Under Auntie's eagle eye we placed the good white china with the gold trim on the table. The battered old silverware box was brought out. The seldom-used silverware was set precisely the way Auntie instructed. She showed us how to make napkin hats to set at each place setting. I've passed this skill on to my children.

The dinner was brought out. Conversations were loud, everyone talking over each other. I often wondered, with all that talking, who was listening? The conversations hummed like a hive of swarming bees. It was a very warm, convivial atmosphere. Dad sat at the end of the table, eating, listening, not saying anything. The conversations circled in and around him, no one engaging him in chatter. He just kept eating. Lemon pie was one of his favorite desserts. Once he had eaten his pie, he moved over to the piano and started playing. He seemed lost in the music. Maybe being surrounded by jolly relatives brought back happy memories of holidays when everyone burst into song. I sure hope he had some happy memories stored. The music seemed to signal dinner was over.

The men moved to the living room and lit up cigars while the women cleared the table. Melodies like "Shine on Harvest Moon" and "Don't Sit Under the Apple Tree" seemed to mellow my father. He'd have a faraway look in his eyes as he played. No words, just the melody ringing in our ears. If we thought it safe, we might sit next to him on the piano bench and request a song. "Daisy, Daisy" was a favorite we all sang along with. Dad couldn't read a note; he played by ear. He'd hear a song on the radio and start picking it out with his right hand. When it sounded right to him, he'd add the chords with his left hand, employing the foot pedals for emphasis. He could play any song. Sometimes little Uncle Eddie would stand beside him belting out verse after verse in his deep tenor voice, crushing the notes of "I'm a Yankee Doodle Dandy" and "The Yanks are Coming." You could almost picture folks in war-torn England singing along. Dad played all the old tunes. Music, whether fun or sad, lifted our spirits, and everyone engaged. Why couldn't music have healed his messy mind?

Some Thanksgivings were full of happy moments to remember.

When I look back on that particular day, the faces are fading. My ears still ring with their laughter, their silly jokes. They were a rag-tag bunch of relatives brought together by my mother's abundant love. The Thanksgiving celebration was more enjoyable because we were together; no one was left to celebrate alone. As my mind wanders around that table, I realize all are gone now; only my sister and I are still here. The memories are stuffed into place, waiting to be pulled out and savored when I want to remember the great Thanksgiving feast.

Chapter 9

Joys of Christmas

We waited eagerly for the first snowfall to soften the bleak landscape, lifting spirits, reminding us of the arrival of Christmas. Just the thought that Christmas was coming diminished sad thoughts.

Around this time of year, Momma always played "Peter and the Wolf" on our record player. After that, it was "Peter Churchmouse." Was she craving the mellow orchestra sounds? Would those melodious notes sooth rattled nerves, paving a stormless path to Christmas? A week before Christmas, out would come these two recordings. I'd lie on the floor, playing with my cut-outs; half playing, half listening to the stories told with music.

Milwaukee sprang into action for the holiday season. Gimbels, once home to the infamous Gertie the Duck, who nested on river pilings outside their window, prepared their windows for Christmas. Both the Gimbels department store and the Boston Store on the next block set up whimsical animated Christmas window displays to entice folks to come downtown: Mr. and Mrs. Santa Claus preparing for Christmas; busy elves making toys and baking Christmas cookies. Noses pressed to the windows, children knew this was how it looked at the North Pole.

A Wisconsin magazine called *Exclusively Yours* came out with a stunning pictorial edition of "Jolly Old Santa Claus." The superb artwork by German artist George Hinke captured what every child knew in his or her heart was the real North Pole. Later in life, my oldest son carried the book around like a Bible, taking it to show and tell so his friends could see what the North Pole looked like. The holiday collectibles company Department 56 has captured the likeness of this book. Later in life, *Exclusively Yours* bought my first article—a story of my young nephew playing football.

Schuster's department store, because it wasn't located downtown, featured a giant toy machine to lure children there. Every child in Milwaukee, quarters clutched in little hands, rushed down the spiral staircase to try their luck at the tall toy machine.

You selected a girl or boy option, and the machine spit out magnificent toys—not cheap Cracker Jack junk.

Milwaukee was a very ethnic town. Many households celebrated St. Nicholas Day on December 5th. My mother, being first-generation American, brought the tradition to our family. Grossmutter, on my mother's side, told me that when she was a young girl, they placed their wooden shoes outside their front door. The next morning they discovered St. Nick had come and stuffed their shoes with oranges, nuts, and candy. Not having any wooden shoes, we hung our ugly long brown stockings on the radiator. The next morning they would be stuffed with tangerines, nuts, candy, and one small toy. One whiff of a tangerine, and visions of St. Nick still dance in my head.

One year, St. Nick paid a personal visit. We were gathered at Uncle George's house—me, Momma, Elaine, Dick, and our Geuder cousins. There was cream soda for the kids. The adults savored brandy Old Fashioneds. Brightly colored trays of assorted Christmas cookies waited for sugar-craving kids to snatch them.

And just like in the story "The Night Before Christmas," we heard such a clatter and wondered what the hell was the matter! There was grunting, a little swearing, heavy breathing and puffing as a window in the dining room was pried open. I screamed. Dick ran to Momma. Elaine stood paralyzed. My cousins clung to their mother. A long, flimsy, red flannel leg came dangling through the open window. It wore white socks and scuffed brown shoes. A slithering, skinny body dressed in an ill-fitting red suit fell through the window. Picking himself up, we noticed a schmutz beard attached to his ears—it sort of covered his mouth. In his left hand he carried a large brown potato sack that bulged in places. A red hat was knocked half off his small head.

"Ho, ho, ho," he shouted, coming into the living room where we stood motionless. Noticing Elaine and me, he ordered, in a gruff voice, "I need to see some tap dancing if you want a gift."

Elaine, always the good kid, leapt into her butterfly routine—her arms flailing and swinging round and round in circles, her toes tapping up a storm. The sound of her tapping feet still resounds in my head. She heard "No toy if you don't dance," and she danced.

I kept screaming. "Stop screaming," Momma laughed as I clung to her side. I stopped, but I didn't dance. No toy was worth it. Dick never moved, nor did my cousins. St. Nick gave up, distributed one toy to each of us, and left by the front door.

We didn't know who St. Nick was then, but we secretly hoped that next year he'd just fill the stockings while we slept. I was young, and I don't know what made my father join in like that, giving us joy instead of sorrow. Wanting to fulfill a kid's fantasy. Maybe deep down he remained a kid at heart. Why couldn't the kindness, buried deep within him, push out the madness?

My siblings and I needed money for Christmas presents, so we sent away for a catalog of Christmas cards to sell. The large folder opened up displaying various cards to order. The three of us would traipse around the block, ringing doorbells, inquiring if anyone would like to order a box of Christmas cards. We sold some and couldn't wait to rush to Radtke's drug store and buy Momma a bottle of Evening in Paris perfume in its beautiful blue bottle. I wonder what Momma did with it. Let's just say it wasn't an Enjoli scent.

Schuster's department store continued to spread joy with a fantasy-filled Christmas parade. No trucks, fire engines, or big balloons— just three long, enchanting Christmas scenes. No one noticed that the floats were white-covered trailer trucks. To our eyes, they were sparkling, snow-covered Christmas scenes. The parade floated down

Vliet Street past Schusters' three-story building. Lucky for us, Aunt Molly lived in an upstairs apartment, right on the parade route. Tante Anna, eager to participate in the joys of Christmas, drove us. We'd pile out of her car, scamper up the steps, say a quick hello to Aunt Molly, and race to choose the most strategic window spot. Noses pressed against the glass, legs twitching, we tried to wait patiently. There were Christmas goodies displayed on a hand-embroidered table cloth, but nothing tempted us to leave our coveted spots at the windows.

My heart began to pound when I saw the glowing lights of the floats come into view. The shimmering floats sparkled with tiny lights, reflecting on the evening's fallen snow. Instantly we were transported into the world of enchantment. One float featured Santa's snow-covered village, houses twinkling with stardust. Another float was Santa's workshop, complete with elves busy working on Christmas wishes. The last float, of course, was Santa, stuffed into his sleigh with six real reindeer (pre-Rudolph). Me-tek the Eskimo stood waving at his side, along with Billie the Brownie. This was the kind of magic Christmas created.

Before Santa flew back to the North Pole to fulfill Christmas wish lists, he visited every elementary school. Teachers kept it a surprise. One afternoon we were ushered out onto the playground. Excited screams escaped our mouths when Santa's float came through the gate. There he sat, Me-tek and Billie by his side, bored reindeer stamping their feet. Santa gave a hearty welcome, reminded everyone to be good boys and girls, and handed candy canes to all.

Billie the Brownie hung around Milwaukee until Christmas Eve. Everyone was encouraged to write Santa a letter, then Billie would reach into the huge grab bag and choose twelve letters to read on the WTMJ radio station. I wrote each year and used my best penmanship. I listened closely each night to hear my letter read, but to no avail. Thousands of letters were sent to the radio station for years. You see, Christmas was not just a day in Milwaukee, it was the entire month of December. Merchants and parents alike ensured that Christmas would be a time for celebration and excitement for all the children—a time of magic.

Christmas Eve day would begin with Dick, Elaine, and I trundling up the block to Tante Anna's house. She always enhanced Christmas Eve day festivities by inviting us to her home. Snowflakes covered our hats and mittens; our tongues stuck out, ready to catch them. I wanted so much to catch one or two or three, to see if each snowflake was different. Never could do it; they melted too quickly. Up the street we trudged past Brenda and Kabeena's house, a Christmas tree glowing in their front window. On the beautiful boulevard in front of our house, the towering, snow-covered evergreens reminded me of tall frosted cakes.

We felt like miniatures captured inside a snow globe. Sometimes Dick and I would run across the street and play on the boulevard, unbeknownst to Momma. We trudged past Hawley Road School. The playground was empty now for Christmas vacation. There's the back fence where I learned about the birds and the bees when Maryellen brought a medical book to show us the birth of a baby, shocking us all into spinsterhood.

"Hello," we shouted to Tante Anna, stomping the snow off our boots as we came in the back door.

"Come in, come in," her joyous voice boomed. "Take off your boots and leave them in the back hall." Cigarette in hand, she motioned us to come into the kitchen.

We did as we were told and hopped up the three steps into her inviting kitchen. Creamy hot chocolate in Christmas mugs stood ready for cold hands, along with platters of sugar cookies and slices of candied stollen (which had a yucky taste to me). This would maintain a good sugar high. Heading into the living room, we saw Tante Anna's squat, round Christmas tree, branches draped with colorful ornaments and sparkly tinsel. With one eye on what lay under the tree, we made our way to the davenport and sat down. Lots of gaily

51

wrapped Christmas gifts were stacked beneath the trunk. We knew there would be a gift for each of us.

Then it was time to make our way back home. Hats, mufflers, boots and gloves on, we hurried back down the street to our house. It was Christmas Eve; nothing would spoil this special day.

As we opened our front door, an overwhelming fresh pine smell sent our senses reeling. In the corner of our front room stood a tall, skinny pine tree. Dad was putting it into the tree stand. You couldn't tell the tree from him, but who cared. I could never figure out how he managed to find a tree and bring it home. Our car was long gone.

Home early from work, Momma was hauling boxes and boxes of Christmas tree ornaments down from the attic. Throwing our coats in a heap, we hurried to help decorate the tree. There were orange and red bubble lights to attach to the tree limbs; a red plastic Santa with feathery beard to hang; red ornaments with pink and silver stripes, round red and blue ornaments filled with silvery stars, miniature cardboard houses with snow-covered roofs, and silver birds with long silver tails clamped to the tree branches. The Christmas light bulbs of orange, red, green, and yellow were large, and would burn out during the season. My favorite part of decorating the tree was the *piece de resistance*, the tinsel. Each silvery strand was hung carefully to cover the pine branches, reminiscent of sunlight on icicles. It was as if we waved a magic wand over the branches, providing a sparkle that twinkled down the ages.

At five o'clock, Tante Anna and Uncle Walter arrived to take us to Christmas Eve services. Elaine and I dressed in matching red velvet jumpers, stitched by Momma, our frilly white blouses completing the look. Our patent leather shoes would not be stuck into boots. Dick had on new beige pants, white shirt, and brand-new red plaid Christmas tie. Momma, bursting with happiness, wore her brown tweed suit and brown pumps. She was always happy when she was going to church. Dad didn't come with us. He watched all the preparations quietly in the kitchen, a cup of coffee in one hand, and in his other brown-stained hand, a cigarette. Did cigarettes calm his troubled mind? I guess we may have asked him, "Are you coming with us?" but it was understood he would not be coming. Rex lay at his feet.

Hearts fluttering, we clamored to get out of the car and into the church. Sunday school kids had to meet in their respective classrooms. Aunts, uncles, and parents were seated in church. At the signal, the organ pounded "It Came upon a Midnight Clear," and all the kids entered the church with their teachers. Two by two we marched down the brown-brick aisle, under the medieval arches to the back of the church. When we turned to descend down the center aisle, shivers ran up and down my arms. My eyes stared in wonderment; my mouth hung open as the magnificent altar came into view. Green pine trees, interspersed with glittering white trees, cascaded across the entire altar. Red poinsettia plants splashed across the front of the communion rail. It was as if we'd slipped into God's splendid garden. I half expected to see God perched on the altar. Upon entering my pew, I twisted round and round, my pigtails flapping in my face, looking for Momma and my aunts and uncles. Reassured they could see me, I tried to settle down, but everyone was bouncing up and down in our pew.

Each class had a special song to sing. The very young always sang "Away in the Manger," complete with hand motions. "Little Town of Bethlehem" was next, and the program ended with everyone singing "Joy to the World." I felt so special to be up front belting out "Little Drummer Boy." You knew each word and note placed you in Bethlehem, gathered around the shepherds and Mary and Joseph watching baby Jesus. I couldn't figure out why I was never chosen to be Mary! Joy coursed through my veins. I knew God heard my voice reverberating through the air waves. The children's cheerful voices filled me with a sense of oneness, enhancing the mystery of Christmas.

Those memories are stored deep in my heart. When the service ended, we kids marched back to the Sunday school rooms. At the door each was handed a red mesh stocking filled with Christmas candy. The kind you never liked—but it was Christmas! I'm sure my father would eat it.

All our aunts and uncles would come to our house after the service. Momma had prepared traditional tartar sandwiches on Milwaukee rye bread, each topped with a huge slice of Bermuda onion—a Christmas delicacy. There'd be stollen, pecan fingers, pfeffernüsse cookies and, of course, our brightly decorated Christmas cookies. We kids spent hours frosting each cut-out cookie, tongues hanging out, licking the frosting-filled knife when no one was looking, competing to create the most perfect Christmas design. Momma's famous eggnog, whipped to perfection and laced with rum, would be served to the adults. Kids got to lick the beaters, but we never tasted the finished product.

Dashing from the car, eager to see if Santa had arrived yet, Dick and I screamed upon entering the front room. Rex lay there, blood rushing out of his nose. "Rex is dead!" we screamed.

Dad was sitting hunched over on the piano bench, smoking. "He's okay," he slurred. "Damn dog ran out in front of a car."

"You killed him!" I shouted in his face. "Rex hates you. He probably wanted to get away from you." I was sobbing now, my hands clenched in tight fists.

By now my mother and relatives had entered the house. Silently they observed the situation, too stunned to react.

Dad, in a haze of smoke, saw everyone entering the house and surreptitiously slunk out of the room and down to the basement.

Dick and I lay down next to Rex, cradling his head, petting him. I looked out the front window. Across the street, Christmas lights were burning; it was Christmas over there. It was Christmas next door at the Fitzpatrick house. It was Christmas on the right at the Meyers' house. Here, at our house, Christmas was over.

Post Note: Rex pulled through; he too was a survivor!

Chapter 10

The Many Versions of My Father

Redeemer Lutheran Church was our safe haven. In the beginning it was a German-speaking church, but during World War II it switched to English. A majestic red-brick example of European Gothic architecture, it stood mightily at 19th and Wisconsin avenues. The inside walls were brown brick; the sides of the church had medieval arched walkways. Filigreed lanterns hung along the sides of the nave. The balcony at the back of the church, above the narthex, held the powerful choir. A pipe organ enhanced their booming voices. The sight of the choir strutting in two by two, looking smart in blue robes with white satin collars, sent shivers up and down my arms; their robust voices straightened my spine. Even if you didn't like singing songs with ten verses, which I didn't, their enthusiasm jolted you upright, kept you standing to the bitter end. Blue stained-glass windows surrounded the upper part of the church. The wooden ceiling hovered 52 feet above the sanctuary. It reminded me of an upside-down rowboat that had tipped over and dumped all the folks into the pews below. Today the church's Facebook page reads, "Redeemer Lutheran, located on the edge of the Marquette University campus, is marked by poverty and promise." Some things never change. Well, they now have beehives on their church roof!

Back then, every Sunday, Momma would herd us off to church. I think in her former life she was a Border Collie; she had the same instincts. Some Sundays, we stood embarrassed on the corner of Wisconsin Avenue, waiting for a ride from passing church members. I felt like Zacchaeus hiding in a tall elm tree. As a teenager, I stood with my back to the street, all five foot ten of me, hoping to become invisible. We could have caught a streetcar on the street behind our house, but some Sundays Momma preferred to wait for a ride. Her inability to drive made getting a driver's license a high priority for me.

Momma converted a portion of our second floor into an apartment, bringing in a variety of renters. It was another source of income—income she would need when my father was in the hospital. A portion of her salary went to the hospital for Dad's care. One family who rented our upstairs apartment had a daughter who had contracted polio in the epidemic of 1947. Darlene's left leg dragged when she walked, and her left hand was frozen at a distorted angle. Years later she told me how much she loved our father. I was astounded, and all ears.

"When you all left for church," Darlene said, "I'd creep down the front steps into your living room. I'd call out, 'Bill, Mr. Geuder, where are you? Let's sing songs together.'"

"Your dad was usually sitting in the kitchen, drinking coffee and smoking one cigarette after the other. He'd come willingly into the living room, sit down at the piano, and begin playing, a lit cigarette stuck in his mouth," Darlene recalled. "Sometimes the ash from his cigarette would fall on the keys, but he kept playing. 'Sit here,' he'd motion to me, right next to him on the piano bench. It made me feel special. And he let me choose the songs. He never used a song book, just played song after song with the two of us belting out the words to 'Daisy, Daisy' or 'Shine on Harvest Moon' or 'K-K-K-Katy, Beautiful Katy.' He knew them all. He didn't always remember the words to the songs, just sort of mumbled them, but I did. I sang with gusto, and that made him laugh. I loved it when you were gone. I had your dad all to myself," she smiled. "He was such a nice guy."

At that time, I was probably wishing she'd have kept him! What would he have been like without his distorted brain cells? What did Darlene receive from him that passed us by? How Dad's tenderness slipped out, unnoticed by us but given to Darlene.

Of course it was morning, and he hadn't stumbled out the door to some bar yet. I tried to picture the two of them, side by side on the piano bench. Where did the music take him? Did the music soften his anger, cover up the mixed-up feelings he held tight inside? Was each note crying out his sorrow, or emanating sounds of joy? Was the music telling his story and we weren't listening?

With Darlene at his side, an enthusiastic audience, did that moment restore memories of when he had played in his band—his twin brother George on the sax, Dad at the piano pounding out "Roll Out the Barrel" as gleeful dancers polka'd round and round the dance floor. If they liked it once, he played it again and again. Music, truly a gift from God! If only each note could have repaired one of his jumbled brain cells. I believe everyone does possess a talent. We are all creative creatures, even if encased in madness.

Older cousins remember days on my grandmother's farm when Dad played song after song and all the kids gathered round him, singing. They serenaded everyone with "She'll Be Coming Round the Mountain," "Goodnight, Irene," or "Jingle Bells."

"No matter what the season, he never shooed us away," my cousins told me. "He always paid attention to us kids."

Children did not hold the importance with adults that they do now, so the fact that my father paid attention to them was big stuff. We were not included in adult conversations, which were mostly in German, anyway. A Sunday gathering could include as many as thirty folks. Not much had changed from when my father was young. Even the staggering stack of dirty dishes was the same.

Another cousin remembers Dad flooding the yard so the kids could ice skate. A glimpse of him providing some fun was enlightening.

Then my cousin, whose father was Dad's twin, whispered softly to me, "I didn't like it when your dad came to our house, because all he did was argue with my dad. When I saw him and Rex coming up the driveway, I wanted to lock the doors."

Just the other day another older cousin revealed, "Oh, your dad was so handsome and so much fun to talk with." She left me with my mouth gaping. I don't remember handsome. I remember dull gray clothing, vacant eyes, thinning grayish hair, and tobacco-stained fingers. "Fun to talk with" left me scratching my head.

I remember an incident at a family party: An adult relative came up to me—I was about 11 or 12 years old—and told me to take my father home; he was out of control. Take my father home? Now, how would I manage that? Someone had brought us to the party. I wish I had said, "Should I use your car?"

My father had empathy for others and seemed to feel their need. On one occasion, I was outside sitting on the front steps, holding one of my dolls. A little girl walked by and looked longingly at my doll. Dad happened to be walking up the block. I don't know if he knew who this little girl was, but he said to me, "Give her your doll. She doesn't have one, and you have more."

It took me a moment to realize he was going to give my favorite doll to this stranger. I stuck my tongue out at him and her, clutched my doll with both hands, and took off down the block. I didn't stop until Dad was out of sight—he and the strange little girl. His compassion for others made us invisible.

When it came to music, Dad and I were on the same page. Saturday nights we listened to the Lucky Strike Hit Parade on the radio. The program played the top 40 songs, with the last song in the number-one spot. We both would venture a guess as to which song would be number one. Dad didn't always like who won. His favorite singer was Kate Smith. "Now that is a voice," he'd tell me. When she belted out "God Bless America," I swear he had tears in his eyes.

Unfortunately for the rest of us, we didn't always share Dad's musical choices. There was one song, which I seem to have blocked out, sung by the Ink Spots. It was something about walking past a door. The music was sorrowful and pitiful, driving me crazy. Dad played the record over and over. I am ashamed to say I stepped on it one day and broke it. He never said a word. Who knows, I may have broken his heart. But it was driving me nuts, and one crazy person in the house was enough!

It was heartwarming to learn that my father provided some joy to others. Maybe those happy hours got him through the day. Who would this person have been had he received help early on? It was heartbreaking remembering the pain and agony of such a broken life. Who was this person inhabited by complicated brain cells? What deep feelings did he harbor? What was he like earlier in life? How did he and my mother get together?

Chapter 11
Momma's Backstory

Looking back, I try to visualize my teenage mother fetching the cows—flapper hair bouncing in the breeze, faded cotton dress, shaggy mutt Lady panting by her side, walking stick in hand, crushing buttercups under foot, scattering meadowlarks at a slow pace, warm smile spreading across her face on the way back to the barn. The cows lumbering with full udders provided ample time for teenage daydreams. What were her dreams? Were they typical high-school fantasies? Some dashing young fella comes rumbling down the highway in his yellow ragtop, whisking her away from squawking hens as she snatches their warm eggs, hands pulling on swollen udders filling the milk pail while she sat on her milking stool? Was she remembering how town kids teased her and her siblings for smelling like sweet silage when they entered the classroom each morning? Did her dream of becoming a teacher waltz out the barn door and into the bright city lights? Did this hardworking, practical girl dream of a different lifestyle for herself?

"What was the attraction to Dad?" I once asked her. She didn't seem like a person given to impetuous actions.

Pictures of my father in his twenties showed a six-foot-tall fella, unruly blonde hair draped over his forehead, rakish smile, twinkling blue eyes—a saucy man about town. He was charming and lived a good life.

"Your dad loved to dance," she remembered softly. "It was exciting, knowing that on Saturday night we'd be twirling around and around under the sparkling crystal chandelier in the George Devine

Million Dollar Ballroom at the Eagle's Club in Milwaukee, or kicking up our heels at the Rainbow Dance Club."

Dad was a smooth dancer; everyone said so. I'd picture the two of them on a Saturday evening—no kids, no responsibilities, big-band music, everyone giddy. Dad clutches Momma to his chest as he guides her around the sparkling dance floor. Their shining faces are reflected in the chandelier lights. I feel her heart pounding, shivers creeping up and down her arms, eyes brimming with tears of laughter, the thrill of being his chosen partner! The excitement he projects, she wanting to remain in his arms like this, waltzing down the highway of love. Life is fun! For a while I do believe it was just that, fun. But how does anyone know what lurks around the next corner, waiting to snatch your dreams? As long as the music kept on playing, Dad kept on dancing. The day the music stopped, so did the fantasy.

My maternal grandmother, Elizabeth Kranz, hailed from Neuenhaus, Germany, near the Dutch border. Oh, how her eyes twinkled with memories of gliding on the frozen canals behind her house. Life changed dramatically when news blew across the ocean. A stern aunt from Illinois decided she needed a domestic helper. The aunt, originally from Germany, sent her pastor to Elizabeth's house to recruit an unsuspecting victim. Elizabeth's mother was a sister of this American aunt. Elizabeth's older sister, sensing the intentions of this pastor's visit, hid under her bed until Elizabeth and the pastor had departed. The trip was presented as a vacation. Little did Elizabeth know it was a one-way ticket.

It was 1899 when my grandmother left her home, her family, her country. Elizabeth was 16 years old and spoke only German, sailing from Bremerhaven to Ellis Island, New York. A huge regret of mine is not questioning her more about this trip. Her two brothers escorted her to the train station and left her there. Departing the train station, she and the pastor boarded the huge steamship to America. She never spoke about that boat ride—too painful to remember. Were there tears as she took her first step on board? Did anyone speak to her on that trip? Standing still, hands grasping the ship's railing, watching her homeland disappear, did she question why she had agreed to this trip? As the tears cascaded into the ocean, waves rolled, her stomach tightened, and her mouth filled with bile. How great the homesickness must have been the minute that ship set sail. What did she bring along? A favorite book, pictures of her parents? I'll never know, because I didn't think to ask her. What a missed opportunity. So many questions I have for her now.

At Ellis Island, Elizabeth's small, black-buttoned boots shuffled along and stood in long lines. Lines to check her eyes, her health … so many questions to be answered. She must have been bewildered. Her traveling bag was chucked among a towering array of suitcases on the waiting trolley. No female could leave Ellis unaccompanied— hence the pastor's presence. Squeezing her small hand in a tight grip, he led her off the island to a waiting train heading West.

The pastor deposited her at her aunt's farm. Elizabeth, excited to tell her aunt all about her voyage, was struck dumb by her aunt's stern voice, "*Schnell, schnell*, don't dawdle. There are dishes to be done."

It didn't take long for Elizabeth to understand why she was at her aunt's farm. Chores were listed, and she would obey.

"Don't try to run away," her aunt snapped. "The police will find you and bring you back here!"

Elizabeth, too meek to entertain such a thought, settled into the situation. Thoughts of, "What has happened to me?" entered her head. She tried school for a while, but the kids all laughed at her German tongue. At lunchtime she had to walk back to her aunt's house to help feed the workers on the farm. This caused her to be late returning to school. The kids at school "always they asked me if I washed the *tisch*," she said. They were asking her about washing the dishes, but it sounded like *tisch*, which is "table" in German. The teacher didn't speak German, so Elizabeth just sat and wrote her name over and over and over again.

"Why did I think this would be a vacation?" she wondered. Picturing her school in Germany and all her siblings made her heart ache. Would she ever get out of this dire situation?

Disappointment and despair disappeared when my someday-to-be Grandpa Schlenvogt arrived to work on her aunt's farm. Emil Schlenvogt Jr. was born in Port Washington, Wisconsin. He was one of 15 children born to my great-grandparents Emil and Emma Popelke, who hailed from Prussia. Emil was 16 years old when he sailed to America, and his future wife, Emma, was 7. Both came to Port Washington with their parents. Neither Emil nor Emma realized they were on the same boat leaving Germany and would one day marry.

"Kathleen," Grandma said. (She called me Kathleen till the day she died.) "When I laid eyes on him, I had a million butterflies flitting about in my stomach. My heart was fluttering! It was love at first sight.

"When he came up to me behind the outhouse, grabbing hold of my waist and twirling me about one sunny afternoon, my cheeks were pink. What if that wretched aunt saw us?" she laughed. "My hands were sweaty, clenched tightly in my apron pocket, when he asked me to marry him. 'Yes!' I shouted."

Elizabeth was 19. Emil was 27. They were married in LaSalle, Illinois, on January 21, 1903.

Off to Wisconsin they fled. Emil worked on someone's farm in Waubeka. They started a family, and money was scarce. They were poor and hardworking, but they reveled in being together. They had one large pot-belly stove in the middle of the room that provided heat for the entire small house. My mother and her siblings were born there.

My mother remembered wild strawberries behind their home, and cherry trees. There was a big gravel pit on the property that the kids played in. Emil never realized that the gravel pit offered potential income. There wasn't a market for gravel then. The next person who bought the house made a great living off selling gravel to folks in need of paved driveways. Timing!

The farm house was so cold in winter that icicles hung from your nose in the morning. "We never changed our long underwear until it was a wash day," my mother recalled. "We wore long underwear all winter long, even under our dresses. We would pull our stockings up and tuck the long underwear into our stockings so the kids at school wouldn't tease us."

Emil helped Elizabeth with English, as he spoke both languages. My mother and her siblings all spoke German and English when they went to school. Once Emil was able to secure a loan, he purchased a small dairy farm in Port Washington. They were ecstatic that this large farmhouse had a huge furnace in the basement that would heat the first floor, with the second-floor bedrooms still a little chilly. Years later, one of my uncles inherited the farm and turned it into a huge dairy concern, milking over 200 head of cattle. Wonder what Grandpa Emil would have thought of that?

My grandmother never returned to Germany. Many a morning she would stand on her back porch, one hand shading her eyes, searching the highway for a dirt-billowing mail truck. Wiping away tears, she tucked her hanky into her bosom. If I happened to be visiting, she'd ask, "Kathleen, would you run down to the mailbox and fetch the mail?" I'd skip down the gravel driveway to the road, thrust my hand inside the mailbox, grabbing hold of the mail—flyers for chicken feed, adverts for milking apparatus and sewing accessories, a church bulletin, and an onion-skinned letter with a foreign stamp. I handed her the mail. Her reddened hands fumbled through the adverts until her watery eyes found the letter with the foreign stamp. Smiling, she slid the letter into her gingham apron pocket. It would be read tonight when everyone was in bed. Tucked in tight in her high feather bed, a tear-stained hanky in one hand, the treasured letter clutched in the other, a shot glass of schnapps on the bedside table, long distances would be reached.

After stewardess training in 1961, the first thing on my agenda was to take Grandma Elizabeth to Germany, where she could reunite with still-living siblings and to see her homeland.

"No, Kathleen," she said when I told her of my plans. "Twice in my lifetime I can't leave my country. If I return to Germany, I will stay there. Now my children and grandchildren are here in America. I'm staying here." She spoke with fondness of the years she spent raising her children and basking in the love of her grandchildren. "Kathleen," she said, "raising your children is the best time of your life," and a huge smile spread across her plump, weathered face. "You go, and remember to look at the linden trees for me—smell them."

I did. My mother and I visited Grandma's childhood home, a little worn looking, beside the canal. I didn't take a photo of it, thinking Grandma should remember her first home as it had been. We saw her red-brick school and her staunch church standing under the fragrant linden trees. The homes were solidly built, so not much had changed except for the murky canal. When I entered the small church, I could picture Elizabeth sitting quietly inside, respectful, as the stern preacher went on and on. She always tried to do what was right. I tried to capture all I saw. We were able to meet her three sisters and a brother. All of them now have hair as white as snow, just like my grandmother.

Tante Mimi laughed as she retold the story of hiding under her bed, hoping not to be found until her sister had departed for America. Mimi wished she could feel her arms around her sister again, see that twinkle in her eyes when she laughed, squeeze her so tight she gasped for air. This would never happen.

Tears were shed as we met for the first time. Everyone inspected these American relatives, seeing if my mother and I measured up. It was bittersweet. I wished my grandmother had been there. Her siblings expressed their gratitude for the much-needed packages sent after the war. I told them how I had helped my mother wrap the boxes, my finger holding the string until it was pulled tight. I also told them how much we treasured the Hummels, the tablecloths, and straw dolls they sent us. I hadn't realized that those treasures had been theirs. It was a humbling moment for me.

Chapter 12

Life on the Farm

My maternal grandmother, Elizabeth Schlenvogt, created a healthy, happy lifestyle for her family. There were chores, but love and laughter, too. My mother milked many cows; she also helped with the baking and gardening. Threshing time was a necessity, to bring in the hay for winter feeding, but also a time for socializing. Farmers from around the area pitched in at each other's farms, quickening the workload. Horse-drawn wagons filled up the driveway, ready to roll. Hayfields lay waiting. The hay was cut, baled, and pitched into the barn's rafters. No horse or cow would want for food.

During World War II, German prisoners of war were sent to work on the Wisconsin farms. The disillusioned young soldiers pitched in to bale the hay; a few lucky prisoners landed at my grandparents' farm. German food and German language must have made them wonder what was happening at home. I remember my grandmother telling me, "Ach, they were such young boys."

During the hot days of August, threshing time, the farmers' wives were busy in the kitchen. Lunchtime found them ladling rich pork gravy into huge bowls. The table was covered with platters of sliced pork and beef, as well as bowls filled with boiled potatoes.

"Grandma," I asked her one time, "why are your boiled potatoes so dry? Do you dry each one with a towel?" That made her laugh out loud. She never did tell me, and I still wonder how her boiled potatoes were so dry. When I boil potatoes in water, they are wet—but not hers.

There were bowls of freshly picked green beans, saucers of sliced, vine-ripened tomatoes, dishes of dill pickles, and plates of home-made bread. Grandma circled the table of ten hungry men, a giant round loaf of rye bread under one arm and a carving knife in her hand, slicing three-inch chunks of bread for each of them.

From the pantry came rhubarb, tart cherry, and sweet apple pies. Strawberry and peach kuchens and mountainous angel food cakes towered over the heavily laden table. Twelve eggs were used to create one angel food cake. The hens worked overtime.

One time, on a visit to Germany to visit her aunts, my mother took an angel food cake that Grandma had baked. She covered it with a hat and placed it into a hatbox—strictly against international travel rules. This was 1961; security was lax, but the guards were curious. When a German security guard in Muenster attempted to open the hat box, Momma rushed over. She slapped down the hat box exclaiming, *"Nein, ein Hut."* He laughed and let her and the cake enter Deutschland.

I never liked angel food cake. The cakes were so high with so little frosting. Only the top of the cake and the long, high sides were frosted. When I complained to my grandmother, she began slicing the cakes in half and filling the middle with luscious buttercream fillings. Better!

After the meal it was back to the fields for the men, leaving a sky-high pyramid of dirty dishes on the drainboard for the women. If Tanta Anna was there, she'd jump up yelling, "First shift!" That meant you got to place your hands in the nice, clean, foamy water with just the cups, saucers, and glasses to wash. Pity the slow-moving slug who lagged in her chair—she got to scrub the endless dirty pots and debris-stuck pans. That Tante Anna was a sly one. She was my god-mother, a woman who knew how to take charge. Growing up in a house filled with perpetual company taught her to disappear and re-appear only when she deemed it necessary.

Grandpa Schlenvogt, my mother's father, was a big guy with large hands and a soft heart. Teasing was his game. His overstuffed chair sat right beside the door that led to the one bathroom upstairs. Either use that door or it was the outhouse for you, complete with Sears catalogs. Try as I might, I was never able to slip past Grandpa without him grabbing hold of me. With one big arm he reached out, pulled me onto his lap, and tickled me until I almost trickled. Only then, as I screamed for mercy, did he let go.

When Grandpa Schlenvogt died in 1950, they brought him in from the fields lying in the back of the hay wagon. He'd had a massive heart attack. This was the first funeral in our family. I was ten years old. I followed my grandmother in line; she reached into the casket, crying, "Oh, *Opa, Opa*," and caressing his hands.

Never having seen a person who had died, I reached in and touched his hand, too. What a shock! I hadn't realized he'd be so cold. That big, warm teddy bear of a Grandpa. I would never touch a dead person again.

Grandma Schlenvogt was a petite, jolly woman with snow-white hair that Auntie always permed and styled. Grandma enjoyed her visits to Milwaukee to shop, which enabled her to primp and preen. One time I lamented how I hated plucking my eyebrows—it hurt! "Oh, Kathleen," she said. "One must suffer to be beautiful."

Although Grandma Schlenvogt had 21 grandchildren and something like 40 great-grandchildren, on birthdays a specially chosen card containing a new dollar bill was sent to each and every one.

When I reflect on Sundays at the farm, I smell the sweet-sour silage in the barn and remember the fun of flinging dessert—the silage—to each stationed cow. And then there was the naughty fun of floating cucumber boats in the horse trough until our uncle charged out of the barn, yelling, "You'll give the horses stomach aches!" as we ran for cover. And always the horrendous, unbelievable stack of dirty dishes on the side sink, making you wish you were a boy!

If I look back far enough, I remember seeing my father walking in the garden, salt shaker in hand, plucking and eating one rosy red tomato after another. No one bothered him as he savored each sun-warmed, ripened mouthful, wiping away the oozing juice. He was always off by himself. He never seemed to pitch in with the barn chores, but he did climb a ladder to pick cherries for Grandma. No one addressed the problem. We just walked around it as if was a part of our daily life.

Chapter 13

Dad's Backstory

My grandparents on both sides of our family came from different areas of Germany. My great-great-grandfather, Georg Michael Geuder, was born in Fuerth. In 1848, Louisa Stern, a Jewish gal, filled his heart with love. His family informed Georg that if he married Louisa, he would have to leave Germany. With his inheritance tucked into his traveling bag, he grabbed hold of Louisa's thin wrist and whisked her away from Bavaria. It was a time of enlightenment, and he was one of the freethinkers, favoring science over religious thought (which certainly carried on through the ages when I found myself marching for justice and equality in my pink pussy hat, hoping my great-great-grandfather would be proud).

Georg became one of the Forty-Eighters—an Achtundvierziger—to leave Germany at that time. Their boat sailed from Bremerhaven to New York City. Shoulder to shoulder, Georg and Louisa stood at the boat's railing, bidding *auf wiedersehen* to their homeland as the shores of Deutschland disappeared forever. What memories did they bring along? Where did they get the courage to leave everything they knew to begin a new life in a strange country, never to return home again?

Louisa's mother and sister left Germany with the couple, helping ease Louisa's sadness. With stars in their eyes, Georg and Louisa said "I do" in New York City, and reached their destination, Milwaukee, in 1849. Wisconsin had become a state in 1848; land there was plentiful and inexpensive. The young couple's hearts were filled with optimism and fear. How risky it had been to leave their homeland to pursue unknown challenges. What kind of work ethic did they possess to venture so far away? Were they more hopeful than fearful that this new land would offer acceptance and untold opportunity?

In 1849, Milwaukee was filled with German transplants. The city contained ubiquitous velvety green parks. A delightful park graced the shores of Lake Michigan. The city also offered quality education for German children, reminiscent of their homeland. The immigrants brought their recipes for good German beer. Many a German beer garden was erected with oompah bands enticing eager feet to polka. Ah, the polka! Is there any dance as lively as a polka?

In Germany, Georg had been a teacher. His vocation changed in Milwaukee when he opened a tin shop. The sign above his shop read "Geuder Geo Stoves and Tinware." The modest building's beginning on Third Street is where the famous Mader's Restaurant now stands. Georg was successful; long-lasting kitchenware made of tin was in demand. It wasn't long before he had 12 employees. Things were going well. Success was in sight. His son, William Geuder (my great-grandfather), began working for his father at the age of 17. He became a partner and began visiting outlying areas as a salesman.

When Georg Geuder died, his son William, who was married to Emma Paeschke, took over as president, and invited his brother-in-law, Charles Paeschke, into the firm. The company then became Geuder, Paeschke and later Geuder, Paeschke & Frey when another brother-in-law joined the business.

Like his father, William was a "freethinker," one interested in science and skeptical of religious beliefs. He wrote poetry and read Shakespeare. Keenly interested in quality education, he was elected to the school board. As school commissioner, he initiated the idea that this position should no longer be nominated by the aldermen, as party politics could influence where a building was erected, the choice of contractors, the purchase of supplies, and the selection of textbooks. William was successful in having this policy changed, which did not make him popular with the Republican party, of which he was a member. Nevertheless, they encouraged him to run for mayor. He lost. With that defeat he announced, "Once was enough." He would stick to what he knew: manufacturing.

William Geuder possessed a love and joy of life. His letters to his daughter were full of silly rhymes and limericks. On a business trip to Baltimore, he wrote her the following lines: "I was walking down a street full of debris, ashes, dirt, and broken windows. When I looked up, I saw the street was called Pleasant Street! I went on to Liberty Street, where the jail sat. It was about noon and I started off to get some dinner. I went through Bacon Street, Omelet Avenue, and Cherry Court. After dinner I was afraid I would run across Kartoffelsalat Street or Erin go Bragh Avenue, so I took a car on Eager Street, and rode out of town."

William's letter encouraged his daughter to travel, and when she did, to pay attention to the sights and sounds of the areas she visited. He encouraged her to have all the fun she could and to look on the cheerful side of life. He reminded her that it is easier to laugh than to cry, and ever so much more comfortable.

William was a board member at the public library and the museum. He was one of the founders of the Milwaukee Industrial Exposition Association. He belonged to many social organizations—the Deutscher Club, the Shriners, the Masons, and others.

William's business grew into one of the largest manufacturing companies in Wisconsin. He held many patents, including one for enamel paint (more about that later). His company produced metal ironing boards, galvanized pails, dairy pails and strainers, candle and gelatin molds, and lunch boxes. (In later years, Walt Disney commissioned the company to make a Mickey Mouse lunch pail. That particular pail was part of a traveling Smithsonian exhibit. Where is it now? The lunch pails were not successful as they didn't include a thermos.)

William was elected to represent Wisconsin at the World's Fair in Saint Louis, but never made it as he died that year (1904). At one time he had several factories in Chicago and Indiana, but they soon closed to focus on just Milwaukee. At its height of success, the company boasted 600 employees. William was very proud of how he had successfully built the company up from his father's small tin shop on Third Street.

William built his family a mansion on Highland Boulevard in Milwaukee. The neighborhood was known as "Sauerkraut Alley," as many successful Germans built their homes in that area. A wide veranda stretched across the front of the three-story Queen Anne structure. When you entered the house, you found yourself in a long hallway with a Bavarian statue on one side and a large deer head hanging above it. A bench stood on the other side of the hallway, next to a small table designated for collecting calling cards. The first floor comprised a music room, a women's parlor, a library with floor-to-ceiling glass-encased bookshelves, and the kitchen. On the second floor were the bedrooms, but it was the third floor I wish I had seen. A remarkable ballroom graced the top floor. Oh, how I would have glided across those gleaming, polished floors in my white satin shoes! On festive occasions, this room would be festooned with bouquets of yellow roses and white lilies. A garland wound around the staircase leading to the ballroom, welcoming many a young suitor or bride and bridegroom.

William's son George (my grandfather) worked at the firm for a while. He was an intelligent man, a chemist. We were told either he or his father held the patent for enamel paint. We never knew the entire story behind this patent.

My grandfather and his brother were alcoholics. I don't know how their behavior affected my great-grandfather. How is it that the first generation works so hard, successful with their endeavors, the second generation carries on, and the third generation squanders it all? I have been told successful manufacturing companies in Milwaukee would open a second factory in the South. The owners would then send their alcoholic sons to manage them. Out of sight, out of mind!

After William died, George was pushed aside—probably because he was unreliable—and Charles Paeschke took control. Mr. Paeschke was a brother of my great-grandmother, Emma Geuder. I think Emma coddled her sons. Her husband William may have been concerned about his sons' alcoholism, but how the problem was handled I don't know. Were other secrets harbored? Was alcoholism the only mental issue? Did my great-grandparents feel the problems would sort themselves out? Were they too ashamed to admit their sons were alcoholics or perhaps mentally ill? No one would talk about it. Sweep the bad news under the carpet. Look the other way. Control the purse strings to keep money flowing to George's family, and his brother's. Would money solve everything? What happens when the money flow stops?

After William's death, Emma visited Rosswein, Germany, the city her parents were from. When she left the U.S., she wasn't feeling well. Her sons, both alcoholics, were making her ill. Her son Willy was given a crate of new clothes to look for work in Chicago. She was concerned that if she remained in Milwaukee, he would quit looking for work and come home to live. Germany felt like a place for her to rest and try to get on with her life. She lamented, "I had enough cares and worries to last the rest of my life, but it seems I'm picked out for it." (Seems this carried on for many of us—problems sans money.)

Emma was wooed and wed by a wealthy industrialist from Rosswein. She remained in Germany and gave up her American citizenship. She was used to living lavishly in an elegant lifestyle. Train rides were first class. Their symphony and opera seats, complete with lorgnettes in hand, were for the well-endowed.

Living in Germany at the start of World War I, Emma was unable to return to Milwaukee. Nor could she access her Geuder funds, which were held by the American Custodian in Washington, D.C. World War I changed her lifestyle drastically.

Emma's letters to her daughter in Milwaukee tell of how quickly life deteriorated. One letter describes her train ride to Berlin. The train was filled with humanity, packages, suitcases, bundles of every kind. No one would offer her a seat, so she plunked her suitcase down in front of the toilet and sat on it!

She wrote, "Germany had to deliver most of the trains, and the best ones, to France after the peace. The trains that remained were in awful shape. We prefer to ride in IV class with the wooden seats. All the curtains have been stolen off the windows, sections of the plush seats stolen. There are no separate compartments for 'women only'. No one is assisting you with luggage." She felt there were no longer gentlemen to help you. Rudeness and vulgarity was the result. "One's four walls are the best place to be."

When confronted by her daughter living in America, who felt 19 years ago life was better, Emma wrote, "I say don't look back. It's just futile because you can't change the past. You only sadden your heart and your head and there is no use in that. The present time presents us with so many riddles, and reality demands so much of us. We have to let the past slip away. To learn to understand the time in which we live and not to compare it with the past. That is our task. Certain cycles have to run their course, no matter how wild they seem. Then it becomes calm again, just like the weather."

In a 1920 letter to her daughter, Emma wrote, "The devil is in charge of our government. General Von Kapp managed with the help of his regiment to topple the government and elect himself a minister president. The working class is so much stronger than the middle class and what came of all this, the war, so many dead."

When asked if she missed the good Wisconsin fish fries, she answered, "Oh, one doesn't forget such excellent meals."

Emma's brother, Charles Paeschke, would withdraw money from her Geuder funds and send her a food draft. She used that money for acquiring otherwise unattainable food items. Emma wanted very much to return to America, but the price of a ticket was too high. Also, she had given up her American citizenship. She would now need a notarized letter from her brother stating that it was urgent for the company that she return, and that she would not be a burden on the state of Wisconsin should she need care.

Emma lamented what the month of May, 1921, would bring regarding war and politics. "If only President Harding would not allow the French to browbeat him as they did Wilson. Wilson was noble when he traveled to France, but when he left there, he was a changed man. They should chase those Frenchmen home. What do they hope to find in Washington, D.C.? Just because of the silly Statue they sent over that time? They should have dropped that into the ocean. Oh well, sponge this part out."

In 1921, Emma returned to the United States with her second husband. They took up residence on the entire top floor of the Astor, one of the finest hotels in downtown Milwaukee. It was once known as the Astor on the Lake. Her money was waiting for her. Her lavish lifestyle was restored. Once again, Emma was a wealthy woman. Worldwide depression didn't seem to affect her pocketbook.

Upon the death of her second husband in 1928, Emma eagerly set out for the Los Angeles area with her son George, my father's father. George left his wife Elizabeth and their five children in Milwaukee. I'm intrigued that Emma never encouraged her son to remain home to care for his large family. She had expressed concern over her son William needing to find employment, feeling he wouldn't do that if she remained available. And now she and her son George set off for sunny California. Strangely, she didn't invite any of George's children, including my father, to accompany them.

There is an entire scrapbook of postcards George Geuder sent home to his family. It seemed he preferred peripatetic trips before he accompanied his mother to California. Cards from Utah, Wyoming, and Colorado encouraged his children to come and see the Rockies. The cards to his wife, sent from lovely hotels and restaurants, described good meals and places of interest and were signed "Love, Pa" or "Love and Kisses, Pa." I wonder how Grandma Geuder felt about that as she was in Milwaukee holding down the fort. Then again, I wonder if she was glad he was gone, him being an uncontrollable alcoholic. Perhaps his disposition with his mother was a pleasant one, but it wasn't with his wife. Secrets continued all through the years until now.

In California, Emma employed a cook, a gardener, a housekeeper, and a chauffeur named Charles to drive the Pierce Arrow. Her new home was close to Sunset Boulevard. Life was grand! Her jubilant lifestyle of elegant luncheons, Moshe golf and visiting friends suited her. She managed to support her children and her grand-children. Her sons were no longer employed; they lived off Emma's funds.

On November 10,1924, Emma once again became a naturalized American citizen, vowing to remain permanently in the United States.

Upon Emma's death in 1934, her son George returned to Milwaukee, celebrated his 50th birthday, stuffed some clothes in a valise and a few thousand dollars into his pocket, and headed for Buffalo, New York, leaving his family again. It was 1935, and the Great Depression was winding down. Why Buffalo? George was a gambler, and Prohibition was over, so perhaps Buffalo was a good choice.

Not long after George left Milwaukee, his wife received a call from a hotel in Buffalo: "Come quick! George Geuder has disappeared." My father and his sister traveled to Buffalo but never found their father. The hotel owner told them that George was mixing with some bad men. Maybe the Mafia killed him; maybe he was robbed and had no identification; maybe he had a heart attack and someone threw his body into the Buffalo River. Whatever happened remains a mystery to this day. My brother and I think he doubled back and died in our attic. We always maintained that the skull lurking in the rafters was our grandfather.

My grandmother, Elizabeth Geuder, was a Zeidler before her marriage to George. My sister gave me the nickname of Kady, which I still use. I wonder if my grandmother would have called me Kathleen or Kady? I'll never know. She died right after I was born. She had brought a crocheted dog to the hospital for me, and 80 years later, I still treasure it.

Elizabeth Zeidler's family members played a critical part in Milwaukee history. Carl Zeidler, her nephew, was called "The Singing Mayor." He was a tall, blonde, handsome bachelor. Women of Milwaukee would swoon at rallies when Carl belted out "God Bless America." Only Kate Smith sang the song more times. Carl was killed in World War II when the ship he was on was torpedoed.

Carl's brother Frank then ran for mayor and served three terms, from 1948 to 1960. Frank, a brilliant, conscientious young man, was a socialist who made Milwaukee a city for everyone. He was instrumental in bringing public TV to Milwaukee, establishing the University of Wisconsin in Milwaukee, and starting the Milwaukee Museum. Frank was a champion of neighborhood libraries, and he helped preserve an appealing Lake Michigan shoreline for all citizens to enjoy. He ran for president on the Socialist ticket in 1976. When Bernie Sanders ran for office, the *New York Times* ran a story stating, "No, Bernie, you weren't the first socialist to run for president. Frank Zeidler of Milwaukee was." It was a good time to grow up in this city.

My Grandmother Zeidler-Geuder's house on Wisconsin Avenue was a hub of activity. When you opened the front door, which was never locked, you were greeted with the rich smell of fresh-baked coffee cake and apple strudel smothered in rich whipped cream, ready to be served. The home had a constant flow of Zeidler-Geuder relatives. It was as if the house had a whirling front door to encourage relatives kvetching together. The Geuder women were the glue that held their families together—another trait inherited by my family. The Zeidler uncles were all musical; if they weren't harmonizing, they were playing instruments. I guess that is one positive trait my father inherited: musical talent. He was constantly surrounded by music. The family gatherings always included music and politics. When my grandmother died, she bequeathed the piano to my father in her will.

Sunday afternoons, the seven Zeidler uncles would march down the street playing songs, singing, and entertaining folks in every neighborhood bar. The uncles' melodic voices could be heard singing at many Geuder weddings held in the ballroom. Perhaps my father accompanied them on the piano.

My father and his brother didn't look alike; they were fraternal twins. Dad was taller than his twin. They inherited the traditional family names of William and George. (My mother broke with tradition and named my brother Richard). Dad resembled our great-great-grandfather, and Uncle George looked like his father. The two of them were joined at the hip, and both were musical: Dad on the piano and George on the sax formed a little ragtag band. I don't think it had a name. Their song of choice was "Roll Out the Barrel."

If I had a time machine, I would go back and see my father in happier times—his fingers thumping out a boogie woogie, his brown-and-white spectator shoes beating time, one foot working the pedal, sweat pouring off his forehead, blond locks cascading over his eyes as he played "There's a Tavern in the Town." Music oozed from his soul. I can almost picture the joy on his face watching couples— girls in their gauze floral dresses, their whirling legs revealing tan nylons with the seams straight; guys in white shirts and suspenders—spinning round and round the dance floor with smiles on their faces. My father was one with the music. The notes lifted him higher and higher to an unforeseen plane. In this fog-covered euphoria, all he could feel was love and joy.

Neither Dad nor his brother ever held down a job. Pampered by their mother and grandmother, they played their lives away. Summers found them swimming at Hoyt Park, strutting their stuff on the high dive and golfing. The two of them would practice chipping golf balls over their three-story house. Uncle George never used more than two clubs, a putter and a driver, and hit so many holes in one he has a plaque at the Bluemound golf course. My father didn't inherit the scientific genes, the political positions, the factory, or the pot of gold. What he inherited were some very tangled genes. In later life he was diagnosed with paranoid schizophrenia. And the next generation starts from zero again.

There were times Dad and George would drive to the factory and demand to be let in. They could have had jobs there, but they felt they were entitled to start at the top as president or vice president. One of their uncles was called to escort the rascals out.

Marriage must have been a jolt for my father, cutting short his swinging lifestyle and thrusting him into reality, responsibilities. No more endless flow of grandmother's cash.

Chapter 14

Each in Our Own Shuffling World

Entering our kitchen, you were confronted with a screen of smoke filling the air. Between gulping strong black coffee and puffing on short Lucky Strike cigarettes, Dad was a permanent fixture sitting at the red Formica table. It was as if that chair had his name on it. Like cows returning to the same stanchion, this kitchen chair seat was worn out from his perpetual tush. The rich, inviting smell of percolating coffee stirred some people's stomach juices, but not mine. I hated the taste of it, but I loved that smell.

If it was summer, we'd tiptoe past him with a quick look from the corner of our eye, and rush outside. If he walked outside, we went inside. We were like a German cuckoo clock, no pun intended. When the clock strikes the hour, one dancer enters by a side door while the other dancer leaves at the opposite door. We looked very similar. *Cuckoo, cuckoo!* Dad's irascible behavior kept us vigilant. We tried to be totally invisible —each in our own shuffling world.

Dad had a favorite bar on Bluemound Road where the owner must have taken pity on him. Often, they hired him to paint some rooms in the attached house. He liked painting. Was it the sense of refreshing dull walls or the feeling of usefulness that lifted his spirits? Too bad they didn't have a piano in the bar. He could have supplied them with songs. Unfortunately, his reward was a frosty mug of beer or two. The bar was within walking distance of our house, easily reached.

Walking home from school with my friends was like a haunted house experience; we never knew what lay ahead. We were laughing, engrossed with each other's tales of the day, when someone jumped out at us from behind a tree. The lean body had been concealed by the tree trunk. We never saw it coming. We all screamed, staring in disbelief, only to realize, "It's Kady's dad!" Legs wobbling, already schnockered, he laughed, trying to inject humor into the situation. "Surprise!" Oh, I was surprised.

Grabbing hold of my friend's hand, I growled and broke into a run. I was so embarrassed that my friends had seen him jump out at us. He mumbled incoherently, shook his head, and stumbled off in the opposite direction. He left my stomach tied in knots, my red face blazing.

Back then my suit of armor protected me from empathy. I wanted him gone, away from me and my friends. The humiliation was too great. He was exposing our secret. I needed him far away.

When we were really young, we had our three beds in the bedroom downstairs. I remember an incident where we had been awoken from a sound asleep by the large storm window being pried open. The shade whipped up, snapping around the roller, and one long, slim, gray-covered leg came snaking over the windowsill.

Fever-pitch screaming erupted from us kids. We all scrambled into one bed, clutching at each other, eyes alarmed, mouths screaming loudly. A slurry voice shouted, "Quiet!" Jumpin' Jehoshaphat! What next?

Momma hurried into our room. That put a clamp on our mouths. We didn't want to know what would happen next, and we probably wished we hadn't screamed so loudly. "*Gott im Himmel, was ist los?*" she sputtered.

"Ah, shit," Dad cursed. "Why didn't you kids shut your mouths?" We wondered the same thing.

As he banged into our beds to get out of the mess he had created, Momma gave him plenty of room to pass by, and he stumbled out the bedroom door. She closed the window, pulled down the shade, and said nothing. We ducked under our covers, covering up our heads, and remained there until dawn's early light.

Our basement was dark and dank with thick gray cement walls. The floor was also cement. In my teen years I decided to transform one basement room into a gathering place for my friends. Using a photo as a guide, I painted a huge dancing cowboy and cowgirl. (Many years later I had the opportunity to visit our old home, and there on the basement walls the Western figures still danced.) Dick and I painted the bathroom door green in honor of the popular song "Behind the Green Door." Dick's son now has the green door in his basement.

I found a $25 jukebox in the want ads. My cousin Georgie, a mathematical genius, converted it from playing 78s to 45s. He and a friend fetched it, sliding it carefully down the steep basement stairs and installing it into our gathering place. It was a thing of beauty. The jukebox had mesmerizing red and green bubbly lights sliding up and down the sides. Where is it now, I wonder?

Late at night, I would tune the radio to Randy's Record Shop in Nashville, Tennessee. It was station WLAC, with William "The Hoss" howling and spinning the tunes. The air waves were full of static; no one cared. There, you could hear rhythm and blues. The words cried messages of injustice, alcoholism, and love lost; each note penetrated your soul. Your body swayed seductively to the blues. These were recordings by black artists whose records were not sold in Milwaukee. It was the first mail-order business in the early fifties. Difficult to believe, but at that time, Milwaukee radio stations didn't play music by black artists. My jukebox played them all. My "cool" friends tuned into Randy's show. The next morning, gathering at the side of the school, we'd question who had heard the latest Howlin' Wolf, Little Richard, or Bo Diddley song.

Perhaps my father felt this release. Perhaps this music eased his sorrows, removed negative thoughts, lightened his burden. I know rhythm and blues alleviated my surroundings. Music is a gift from the universe.

The irony of all this was that in 1929–1932, more than 20 years before I got my jukebox, the small village of Grafton, Wisconsin, set up a recording studio in the Wisconsin Chair factory. This was Depression time, and the factory owner developed the idea of supplying records with their record cabinets. Son House, Charley Patton, Ma Rainey, Blind Lemon, Louisa Brown, and Willie Brown made their way from Mississippi to Grafton to record some sides. Eddie James House Jr., known as Son House, recorded ten songs for what was called Paramount Records, for which he received $40. There were no royalties. The artists received 78-rpm discs which they could distribute and get their names out at various clubs, house parties, picnics, and the like.

Paramount Records gave black artists an avenue to record. Approximately 25 percent of the nation's "race records" were recorded there. The chair factory employed more than 100 people, and the employees cranked out more than a thousand records per hour.

Grafton, Wisconsin now sprouts memorials to the beginning of the Delta Blues Trail, with a Blues Plaza in the center of the village. The Plaza is in the shape of a piano. Each black and white key sports the name of a blues singer who recorded at Paramount Records. A six-foot blue and black trumpet player graces a fountain reminiscent of the Delta area. The city offers a Paramount Walking Tour showcasing the beginnings of Paramount Records with the hope of establishing a blues festival. I was never aware that Paramount Records existed so close to my grandmother's farm as I listened to Randy's Record Shop in Nashville, Tennessee.

One pleasant summer evening, a few friends came over for a game of cards. We set the card table against the wall under the basement window. Halfway through the game, the window rattled and shook. It wasn't Jerry Lee Lewis singing "Whole Lotta Shakin' Goin On" from the jukebox. It was the window above the card table. The cards fell off the side of the table. Mouths hanging open, we watched in disbelief as two lean gray legs ending in white socks and black shoes slid through the window and crashed onto the card table. Dad was schnockered. The miasma of alcohol clung to his sweaty body.

"*Oy gevalt*, you *schmuck*," I sputtered. "Don't deal him in."

The kids laughed, trying to cover up their embarrassment, gripping the table to sustain the weight of Dad's long body.

Dad loved to play cards, especially the game of Schafkopf, a.k.a. Sheepshead. We were playing Hearts, not that it mattered. I had no intention of dealing him in.

"Game over," I said, grabbing everyone and shoving them up the stairs and out the door. I didn't want him anywhere near my friends. My adrenalin was running rapidly. Humiliation spread through me like goose shit. My heart was pounding, my eyes bulging with rage. I shoved and pushed my friends out the door, trying to erase what had just transpired. I never wanted anyone to know my father was mentally ill. The stigma of mental illness was too raw to confide to anyone. It was built into the fabric of our life. Now he had exposed his illness to my friends, but they never mentioned the incident, at least to me.

Sneaking back toward the fruit cellar, Dad never uttered a word.

What the hell was with him and windows? Did he think no one would notice him coming home? Damn good thing we didn't have a milk chute. We probably would have had to call the fire department to extract him!

When the Braves came to Milwaukee in 1953, enthusiasm was at fever pitch and the city built a baseball stadium for the new team. The county stadium was within walking distance of our house. You just walked through Soldier's Home, a veteran cemetery, and down the hill. The stadium was built on an old garbage dump. The paucity of security made it easy for us to sneak into games. My friends and I loved creeping in under the fence. Once inside, who should we see sitting in the bleacher section? My father! Legs crossed, lit cigarette in his right hand, a cup of Miller in his left, absorbed in the game. He hadn't seen me, so I steered my friends out and around him. We rushed to watch hammerin' Hank Aaron smash home runs with bases loaded, or Billy Burton stealing to second or third. "Run, Billy, run!" we'd shout. Baseball games were exciting.

When security tightened, we had to wait until the seventh inning when the gates opened and you could walk right in. Dang if Dad hadn't discovered that fact. When the Milwaukee Braves won the World Series in 1957, Miller High Life set up wooden sawhorses laden with huge kegs of beer. It was safe to say that the streets were foamy with Miller beer (Molson/Coors came much later). Baseball, brats, and the Braves showed NYC how to celebrate a World Series win Milwaukee style! And Dad was there celebrating.

Chapter 15

Life in Shambles

Our reality was the good days when Dad was gone all day. We never asked where he went; we were just glad he wasn't home. You get what you get and you don't throw a fit.

Life was messy. We knew we were different, but we lived in and around the obstacle that was my father. We didn't expect miracles. Perhaps we wished he'd disappear, but it was what it was, deal with it! When he looked at us with his cloudy, pale blue eyes, I wonder what he saw. Did he know we cried in our sleep? Did he know he disrupted our lives? Did he care?

When he was home, he was either playing the piano or sitting at the red Formica kitchen table, head shrouded in a cloud of smoke, tobacco-stained fingers holding that Lucky Strike until it was a tiny glowing ember. How he didn't burn his fingers is beyond me. Well, maybe he did but was numb to the pain. The other hand brought the white ceramic coffee mug to his mustached mouth for one more gulp of strong coffee. Caffeine and nicotine, his daily nourishment. The coffee pot simmered all day long. At least he was cognizant enough to turn the stove off when he left. Maybe he muttered something to us, I don't know. He could be funny at times. If he was hostile, I'd have a sharp riposte in response.

The bad days were when he'd come tripping through the back door, teetering off balance, swearing that someone had stolen that damn patent. God, how I wished that whoever stole the friggin' patent would return it to us. What damn patent? The enamel paint patent. Great-Grandfather Geuder had many patents under his belt, but for some reason Dad was stuck on that patent for enamel paint. I'll never know the reason for that. When he was drunk, slurring his words, yelling for Rex, even Rex hid. Such a smart dog! We would scatter out the door, waiting for the neighborhood kids to come out and play. We never revealed the turmoil in our house. Remember, it was a secret, never to be disclosed. The words "Our dad is mentally ill" would never be spoken. Never.

Many a day, my sister and I, returning from dance class, would get off the streetcar and take the shortcut home through the back field. No matter how many times we found this gray-clad Dad lying in a fetal position, embedded in field grass, it made us cringe. Sucking in my breath, I was about to speak when Elaine held her finger to her lips. "Shhh," she whispered. "Don't wake him." We'd cut a wide berth around our passed-out father, eager to sneak past him and home. I always took one more long look. Flies sitting on his head, he none the wiser. My eyes moist, knowing this was our father. Our job was to survive and hide.

As the years passed, Dad gave up even the pretense of working. He demanded money to spend at the bar, and Momma gave it to him—a quick solution to an ongoing problem. His mind was on overdrive, literally driving him more insane. The twisted, distorted thoughts consumed his every waking moment. There was a judge who lived a few blocks away. This judge had been responsible for committing Dad's twin brother for alcoholism. After treatment, Uncle George never drank again. He returned home and led an untroubled life, standing by my father until he died. In fact, despite his good health, Uncle George died two weeks to the day after my father's death.

Why couldn't this treatment have helped my father? I guess because Dad was mentally ill *and* an alcoholic. This incident, his brother being committed, was what set off the "someone poisoned my beer" episode. The shock of his brother being committed for treatment was too much; severing their ties was unbearable. In my father's mind, this judge was an enemy. I never knew that many nights he stood in front of the judge's house snarling, "I'll get you, you son of a bitch!" while shaking his fist at the house. The kid who lived there could have bullied me at school but never did. I discovered this about my father at my ten-year high school reunion. I was amazed. Different times, different folks in the White House.

Chapter 16

Life Tears Apart

The finale came in 1953. Who knows what set off Dad's intense rage. Maybe everything came crashing in on him. Maybe voices were screaming at him, reminding him of all he had lost. The fact that he had no control over his life, the feeling of helplessness, uselessness, fed his terrible anger. It was a doozy of an explosion.

It was evening. Supper was over and Dad hadn't come home yet. That meant there wasn't any food in his system when he banged rapidly through the front door. He exploded. Uncontrolled anger spewing from his twisted mouth. Shouting, "I want to know who stole that patent, that son of a bitch, that cocksucker. I'd like to smack his front teeth out."

He slammed into the hallway wall. "I know it's in this house. Someone's been hiding it." Over and over, he ranted about how he was cheated, his family besmirched, all because some son of a bitch stole the enamel patent. His eyes were dark, penetrating, wild, searching … for what? If he could only locate the patent lurking somewhere, all would be fine.

"Get out of my way, Olga," he snarled at Momma, who had jumped up to see if she could appease him. She backed into the piano bench to give him room.

"Bill, what's the matter?" she asked, voice quivering.

"Shut up. What the hell do you know about it?" he growled at her with his fists ready to swing out. Momma flew up the front steps to fetch her brother Ervin, now living upstairs.

We three kids grabbed hold of each other and made ourselves

small in the corner of the kitchen. Rex sprinted away.

Uncle Ervin clambered down the front stairway. Into the chaos, he cried, "Bill, Bill! What is the matter?" hoping to calm Dad down.

He reached out, thinking he could restrain Dad. But Dad wasn't having it. Beyond consolation, he lashed out and punched Ervin in the face. He was like this pugilistic Cassius Clay, swiftly throwing punches left and right. Uncle Ervin, no slouch, probably with learned behavior from his bootlegging days, slugged back. Plants tipped over, dirt was flung into the air, a lampshade flew off. Someone grabbed the light pole, but it crashed to the floor, light bulbs exploding. Momma's *tchotchkes* were knocked off the end table. Down the two of them went, slugging, punching, rolling over and over on the floor. My father was screaming as if he were being tortured. Uncle Ervin shouted, "Call the cops, now!"

Momma raced back upstairs and called the police. The two bodies crashed into the piano bench, kicking it over on its side. My father, full of pent-up rage, kept on slugging Uncle Ervin. Punches kept coming from both sides.

The cops came tearing up the front steps. Two huge boys in blue peeled my uncle off of my father. They grabbed Dad, righting him on his feet. Each cop took hold of one of his swinging arms. They tied his arms behind his back.

"Let me go, you sons of bitches!" came the primal scream of terror. They dragged Dad out the front door, his toes just grazing the steps, and pushed him into the waiting squad car.

This time I didn't yell, "Don't hurt my Daddy!" This time we stood numb to what had just transpired, staring at the disappearing taillights of the police car rushing down Wisconsin Avenue. Fear overcame us. Hands clutched the hems of our shirts and blood pounded in our ears as we tried to process the chain of events.

Dirt was swept off the living room floor. Bits of scattered ivy were picked up and discarded. The lampshade was returned to the lamp. Momma sobbed into her handkerchief. We wondered how much more madness she would have to endure. Rex slunk back upstairs. Words were hushed as everyone tried to console my mother.

That was the day final plans were set in motion. Uncle Ervin drove to the hospital to commit my father. One of Dad's sisters co-signed his commitment papers and lived in fear that one day my father would retaliate against this action. She never wanted to be alone with him again. Like sad sacks, we tried to ascertain what to do next. How did we arrange our lives now, in this latest life episode? Life was such a *gashmeer*.

My father was committed to the Milwaukee County Mental Institution in 1953. I was 13 years old.

Chapter 17

Life Re-Calibrate!

Shaken, we walked around our house. Did we sleep easier that night? No, I don't think so. A child's love is indescribable. We were relieved that the violence had not involved our mother, but sadness was creeping in and slowly crawling over us. What did this mean? We had learned to adjust our lives according to what we had been dealt, but now we were faced with a new unknown.

I saw Dad's scared little-boy face screaming in pain, staring out the back window of the patrol car, and I wanted to scream, "DON'T hurt my daddy!" No words came out, just relief that the police had rescued us. How life continues to snarl your innards. So many conflicting feelings racing through your body. Most of all, a buried love, even though you didn't know you felt it at the time. It was there, waiting to resurface one day. You want to love that person even though anger coursed through your veins. What would happen now when he returned home? I know Elaine, Dick, and I were clueless about what the next chapter would bring. How would we adjust to what had happened? What were our lives going to be like now?

This time my father didn't come home right away. He had been in the hospital before, but only for a few weeks before he rejoined our frenzied life. Committing him to the mental hospital this time would be a permanent situation. He would be allowed to come home every weekend, and getting him back to the hospital would always be a crapshoot—this was our new normal for the next 25 years. Pick up our father on Saturday morning and return him to the hospital on Sunday night. Easy, right? Life was never easy for us.

I marvel at my mother's strength. Where did it come from? She was the tree, the foundation. We kids were the branches that enfolded her. Life's situations had provided us with a shield of armor. We were an unbreakable force. Momma wore her responsibilities like a garment never shed. Just like our Grandmother Geuder, she was the glue that held her family together.

The Native American Omaha tribe says, "It takes a village to raise a child." Support has to come from many. It also takes a village to sustain a helpless family. Momma could have divorced Dad, and we'd have had a more peaceful life. Where would that have put Dad? Out on the streets, homeless? The support of Momma's siblings, friends, and children gave her the nourishment she needed to face life's struggles.

Momma supported us with her income from Allstate Insurance—not quite the life she had envisioned. She injected fun and humor into a dull, routine job. Coming dressed in Grecian garb was one solution to an ordinary Friday workday. Perhaps she never faced the fact that Dad was mentally ill. Whatever works. Whatever she told herself, or didn't tell herself, kept her functioning. I never heard her say those difficult words, "Bill is a paranoid schizophrenic." Her reply to, "Where is Bill?" was "He is ill and hospitalized."

One would think after working an eight-hour day Momma would return home, kick off her shoes, and mix a brandy Old Fashioned. Not if her church needed someone to cook for a hundred folks! Three p.m. in the church kitchen, basting turkeys, mashing potatoes, steaming green beans, whipping up egg whites for her infamous Schaum Torte, Momma was re-energized. Cooking released her creativity. The parishioners' applause sustained her.

Now that my father was in the hospital, Momma had breathing room. Quiet evenings awaited as she retreated to her backyard sanctuary. She loved the cathartic experience of watering her prize geraniums, nourished with cow manure from our grandmother's farm. The double pink and red peonies and bunches of bleeding hearts enveloped her. The knowledge that no one would come crashing through the door released a sense of peacefulness. Her garden provided a modicum of contentment.

We returned home from school knowing no surprises lingered behind a tree except a squirrel or two. The windows were for letting in cool breezes, not long, slithering legs. The field was empty except for a pick-up game of baseball.

Your life relaxes its grip for a spell, but keeps you in the loop of those with heavy burdens to carry. (Like my great-grandmother said, life also picked us for continued problems.) Life for some can be like riding out an avalanche. It can either bury you, or you safely ski out of danger, able to face another day. Shaken but wiser, you are more aware of the pitfalls that remain. Only illusions are swept away.

Every weekend we brought Dad home. This was always a Cracker Jack event; we never knew what version of Dad would be waiting for us at the hospital entrance. Some Saturdays, if Dad was angry, he'd sputter, "Not taking these son of a bitch's pills," and into the bushes the pills flew. Or the times he left the hospital, pills in hand, and squished them on the cement. Or when he announced, "I told them son of a bitches, take them pills and shove them up your ass. You need them more than I do."

"Oh, it's going to be one of those exciting weekends," I'd say to myself. It's rock and roll time. Do not be planning anything special. That would be a weekend where Dad would find his way to a favorite local bar to have a few drinks. Not good when taking medication, but oh, right, he threw those pills into the bushes. No problem there. There'd be some mumbling and incoherent chatter, but no violence.

He seemed hungry for familiar food as he devoured bowls of chili. Lucky Strikes returned the blue haze in our kitchen. If the cousins were hosting a family gathering at Hoyt Park, he silently came along. Everyone gave him space. He remained at a picnic table watching, listening, and smoking. You could see his mouth moving as he talked to himself, but nothing loud or offensive came out of it. It's not like anyone ignored him; they just never engaged him in conversation. Well, maybe they engaged him a little.

Come Sunday night, he reluctantly got back into the car and returned to the hospital.

As time marched on, he grew a little more accepting of the fact that he had to return to the hospital. Of course there were exceptions. We were never confident that the catastrophes were over. There were weekends when we held our breath. Would he curse and swear but amble into the car, returning to the hospital on Sunday evening?

Good behavior resulted in weekends home and sometimes a longer visit. My sister remembers an incident when Dad decided he wasn't returning to the hospital. It was going on seven days, and Momma and Elaine were exasperated. If he didn't return within eight days, he would have to be committed all over again. Sometimes God isn't too busy to notice a crisis looming. Dad took the streetcar down to the courthouse. We think he planned to negotiate his release. The police at the courthouse discovered he lived at the county hospital and politely provided him an escort "home." Crisis averted.

Later, he would tell his grandchildren that life at the hospital was filled with flatulence. "I have to smell all those guys' farts," he said. "Every day. They should have an outhouse." The bathrooms didn't have individual doors on them, just rows of toilets. That, of course, tickled the kids. Dad said the constant yelling of other patients made him want to cover his head.

Our lives continued, peppered with unexpected surprises. There was the time Dad entered the hospital and quickly stepped back out carrying a radio. "Wait," he shouted to us. "Give this to Jenny," my daughter, his granddaughter. In big black letters it was stamped "Property of Milwaukee County Hospital." When he returned inside, we threw the radio into the bushes. Life kept us vigilant.

At times Dad accepted the fact he lived at the hospital, or at least felt helpless to change the situation. Maybe he thought it was his fate, I don't know. I know we felt protected with him in the hospital. The Milwaukee County Mental Institution was the greatest anodyne in our shattered lives. He lived there, on and off, for 25 years.

When I married in 1962, I asked Dad to walk me down the aisle. He said no, he couldn't do that, but he did come to my wedding. My godfather did the honors. At our wedding reception, Dad surprised me as he ambled over and held out his arms to me. His bony body was encased in an ill-fitting gray pinstripe suit and my brother's blue tie. His worn out, life-weary face, sunken gray-blue eyes ringed with lines, contained a slight smile. His arms embraced my body as we graced the dance floor. He was still a smooth dancer, moving easily with the music. All of a sudden he leaned in close and began singing in my ear, "You are my sunshine, my only sunshine."

I was stunned. His words stirred something in my heart. I was utterly flabbergasted; this unforeseen development suspended my dance movements. For a fleeting moment, the serendipitous gesture softened my feelings.

What did this mean? Why was he singing this song to me? I harbored so much anger. My feelings were a jumbled mess. I'm not sure I ever thought he loved us. Weren't we all just surviving, and love was for the more fortunate? What was he feeling? Was the medication lessening his anger? Had he harbored moments of love for me? I have no idea. For one fortuitous moment, I felt anger dissipate with the realization of how this disease had robbed us. What life might have been. A child's love remains open, always hoping for a better day.

As a kid I sometimes asked him, "Dad, what do you want for Christmas?"

"A pine box," he'd say.

"Dad, what do you want for your birthday?"

"A pine box," he'd reply.

"Dad, what do you want for Father's Day?"

"A pine box," he said.

Sometimes I just gave him a carton of Lucky Strikes, snitching a few packs. He'd laugh and say, "Hey, some are missing." He felt he was taking up space and often said he should make room for someone else. "Let someone else take up my space" was a regular refrain.

Life isn't fair; you get what you get and you don't throw a fit. My father taught me that lesson over and over.

In his 25 years living at the Milwaukee County Mental Health Institution, my father lived in every building connected to the facility. Misbehaving, belligerent behavior would place him on a locked ward and deny him access to a weekend pass. Most days he was free to come and go as he pleased. There was an incident where he was caught smoking in the bathroom, which was *verboten*. The punishment: remain in your pajamas all day. Next thing you knew, there he was walking down Watertown Plank Road in his p.j.'s, going to buy cigarettes. Conformity was not one of his strong points, nor was modesty. Had they taken all his clothes, I have no doubt he'd have walked naked to buy his cigarettes.

The Milwaukee County Mental Health facility was set back from the road. There were three large three-story buildings. Each floor included a screened-in porch where the patients could sit. The patients lived three or four to a room. If I visited Dad on his ward, we would sit down near the enclosed porch. The wooden floor was worn and scuffed. The walls of the ward were plain, dull white. There was no color anywhere inside. The building was as worn out as the patients inside.

Sometimes a patient would be on the second-floor screened porch and see me pull up in my car. He'd yell, "Hey, where did you get your license, in a Cracker Jack box?"

Outside there was a sanctuary garden that the patients had helped construct. Bright yellow dandelions sprouted here and there on acres of cool green grass. Large maple and oak trees shaded the front of the facility. A man-made pond lay at the bottom of the lawn, complete with wandering ducks, inviting one to daydream, calm your scattered mind, and breathe in connectedness to a higher power. It was called Healing Gardens by the staff.

When my children were young, we would visit with their grandfather outside on the grounds. He was very protective of them. If patients whom Dad felt were unstable came too close, he would shoo them away. When my kids were babies, Dad would hold them and croon little ditties into their ears. The pleasure of hearing a baby's laughter, their total acceptance of their babbling grandfather, made his vacant eyes sparkle. The older kids would chase the ducks or feed them crusts of bread. Now and then they'd race past Dad and wave. He'd laugh at their energy, not budging from the bench we shared. He would devour a box of chocolate-covered cherries we had brought.

My daughter, who was young when I took her to visit her grandpa at the hospital, said there were several memories that stood out in her mind. The buildings reminded her of how hospitals looked in horror movies. "There were big windows and metal beds with curtains around the bed. I never wanted to be too far away from you, because that's when bad things happened to people in the movies. I never knew he was mentally ill. I thought he was just very, very, sick, and that's why he was in this hospital." (We never explained nor talked about why their grandfather was in the hospital.)

It was the secret we held, shut out from everyone.

"I remember he would just show up at our house and sleep on the couch under an orange afghan blanket Grandma Martin made me," my daughter continued. "He always had on those same gray pants, white shirt, and yellow-orange button-down sweater. I couldn't figure out why he never changed clothes. He wouldn't come to the table and eat with us, either. He'd stay a few days and then *poof*, he'd be gone again.

"He always sat in the same chair at Aunt Elaine's house, next to the window. There would be an ashtray with one lit cigarette in it. You always told me, 'Go say hi to Grandpa,' and I would go in with hesitation. He looked kind of spooky to me, like Vincent Price spooky. I know I was safe, but he looked spooky. I would walk in slowly, and he'd motion for me to sit on his lap. I dreaded that, as his legs were so bony and his hands were boney and wrinkly and his fingers so yellow from nicotine stains. He'd mumble something I couldn't understand, but I would pretend to understand him and agree. After three minutes he patted me on the back and you would rescue me, and I'd run to catch up with my brothers.

"One time, you told me we had to swing by the hospital and see Grandpa. It was summer. My brother Chris was with us. We walked up the big stairs to the main entrance to the building. I remember thinking how pretty the grounds of the hospital were; like a park, fresh-cut green grass. Then, when we got inside, it was all old sick people. I wondered why they weren't outside on this hot, sticky day.

"Grandpa was lying on his bed in his underwear, and he was, oh, so very thin. He was so tall and thin he looked like a stick lying there. There was a fan overhead, and maybe the window was open. You brought him a carton of cigarettes and laid them on the metal table by his bed. I don't remember what you talked about. I know we didn't stay too long, and I think you rewarded Chris and me with a custard at Gilles."

There were days he was very lethargic.

"The last time I saw Grandpa, I was 11 years old," my daughter remembered. "We were on our way to Detroit and stopped at the hospital to see him. This time he was in a different building. He had on a light-blue faded bathrobe and slippers. He didn't look so skinny then. Our whole family came to see him. He was in the activity room, sitting by the wall, and other men were there, too. An orderly found six chairs, and we all sat around him. I remember I had on my long purple coat with the fur collar. Someone started singing Christmas songs, and so did Grandpa, so we all joined in. I sat next to you and Dad. We didn't stay too long. We were on our way to our other grandparents' house in Michigan. The next day Grandpa died."

On one of my visits, I noticed a piano on Dad's ward and told the station nurse she should have him play it. She said they had asked him, but he didn't want to play.

"How come you don't play the piano anymore?" I asked as we sat under the shade of the large sugar maple tree.

"I can't hear the music anymore," he said with a faraway look in his opaque eyes. The medication he was on had mellowed his personality but robbed him of the notes he once heard playing in his head.

Every so often we shared a pleasant conversation remembering how he'd played in his ragtag band and danced the night away, waltzing until his feet were sore, polkas leaving holes in his socks. He shared the words of the song "Dancing with a Lady with a Hole in Her Stocking," bringing a smile to his worn-out face. Saner moments eased some of the hard feelings I had stored.

"What was it like growing up in the Clubhouse?" I asked.

"I can't remember," he said. "There were always so many people in and out. I don't know what we did. My father was gone a lot." He never elaborated on his childhood, nor did any of his siblings.

"My dad liked to travel," he said. "I always wanted to see springtime in the Rockies." He remembered the song that made him want to visit the Rockies. "My dad said I should go, but I never did," he whispered. "Maybe someday I will."

"My father told me I should see Bakersfield. The rows and rows of vegetables. I always wished I could have," Dad said wistfully. A yearning smile brought the knowledge that this would never happen. A sense of sadness prevailed as I took in his long, slender body hunched over on the park bench. His belt was wrapped tightly around his waist, holding up his Sears work pants. His scrawny shoulders protruded through his shirt. His skinny legs were crossed, revealing white socks and dull brown shoes.

His hair was thinning now. His eyes were almost colorless; smudged glasses perched on his straight nose. It was difficult to picture him as an energetic, dashing man around town, women admiring his good looks and fun personality. I imagined him in his spiffy polished dancing shoes, sweat-soaked shirt, and loosened tie, pounding those ragtime piano tunes and singing with gusto, encouraging everyone to get out there and "shake like your momma's not watching!"

Knowing there had been times his clogged mind was free of anger and distortion made me wonder what he had been like, hoping fervently that he had been happy. Our peaceful conversations stirred up so many memories. I found it hard to differentiate what I was feeling, figure out how to readjust. My memories of a fun father were so faint and so very long ago. I had been too young to recall most of the good times.

We lived our lives with the knowledge that we would bring our father home on weekends. It was either my sister or me; my mother was left off the hook, but really, he preferred to be around his grandchildren. We never discussed who would fetch Dad for the weekend; remember, his condition was a secret that was never discussed. Our father's mental state was just a part of our lives. It was like going to the grocery store, but this time pick up your father. Dick wanted nothing to do with Dad; he harbored many dark memories of the verbal abuse he had grown up with. His hatred for our father never lessened. At Dad's funeral, my brother said, "This is the happiest day of my life." And one of Dad's sisters felt the same as my brother—glad that Dad was gone.

There were some difficult weekends. If Dad was in a bad mood, you shuffled through the hours until you returned him to the hospital. The mental institution provided my siblings, my mother, and me a respite from the heavy duty of managing Dad's mood swings. It gave our families moments of a near-normal lifestyle. Our children didn't have to watch us endure the constant pain we saw inflicted on our mother. When I've asked my sons what they thought about their grandfather, they told me he always looked sad, but they harbored no ill will toward him. They didn't understand what was really wrong with him.

Dad was always at birthday celebrations, sitting quietly, watching from the sidelines, ready to devour a piece of his favorite chocolate cake. I never knew how he felt about these celebrations. He never commented, but he did like to be a part of them. He was never left to dwell at the hospital during the holidays.

A building with ramps was the last place Dad lived in. Leaving here wouldn't require stairs. The night he died, an attendant sat with him through the night. He was the last person to be with my father. At Dad's funeral, the young man brought some of the patients who had been on the same ward. I thanked them all for coming, and especially the attendant who sat with Dad as he passed.

"I liked your father," he said. "He was always a gentleman. We talked about music, and he was so humble. He seemed so appreciative of anything I could do to ease his discomfort—get him water, sit by his side. Your dad passed away peacefully." He smiled reassuringly at me. "Bill was ready to go."

I was sure of that, remembering his numerous requests for a pine box.

But ... a gentleman! I had difficulty with that word. It would take years to soften the dark feelings I harbored. It would take time before I could picture my father differently. What did the attendant witness that we never saw? Was this what my mother had experienced on her first dates? A gentleman, happy, relishing life? Kind, peaceful?

A schizophrenic trying to ease his maddened mind with alcohol—that's the person forever etched in my mind. It was forty years before I could even utter the words to new friends: "My father was a paranoid schizophrenic and an alcoholic." Secrets are difficult to speak out loud. What would people think of us if they knew our secret?

Wouldn't you think that his one request to be buried in a pine box would have been honored? It wasn't. You get what you get and you don't throw a fit.

Chapter 18

The Messiness of Life: Who are the Homeless?

It was a blue-sky morning in Denver, as most Colorado days begin. I was just about to add two eggs to a cake batter when the news came on TV. There was President Ronald Reagan smiling broadly. I paraphrase what Reagan said: "Today, I am closing all mental health facilities. Folks can now make their own decisions about whether they want to be in the hospital."

My spatula caught in the beaters; cake batter flipped out of the bowl and splattered all over as I listened with horror to President Reagan's unbelievable statement.

"Closing the mental institutions? Is he nuts? People can choose for themselves if they want to be in a mental health facility?" I kept screaming at the TV. I thought I'd heard it wrong. I didn't. He did close all the public mental health facilities and threw the folks out on the street. The closing of these institutions will forever be attached to his name.

So many of the homeless you trip over on your way to the theater or cafe are mentally ill. The streets are now housing the mentally ill. Maybe 50 percent of the homeless are mentally ill. Studies showed that the deinstitutionalization movement caused this chaos. How many mass murderers are mentally ill? Folks with no one to care for them and nowhere to go have no protection from thugs who think it's cute to beat them up or steal their meager possessions. Without medication, these folks remain untreated. Many of the former patients can't afford treatment, and most don't even realize they need medication. How many mentally ill folks are in prison? Prison! They don't belong in prison.

I had an opportunity to visit a women's prison in Denver. The church I belonged to asked for volunteers to visit this prison for a worship service conducted by inmates. Six of us went. It was a Friday evening, and the prisoners could have gone to a movie, but instead wanted to conduct a service with their young chaplain. They wanted folks from the outside to attend.

The prisoners led the service. There were 12 of them, the chaplain, and us. It went smoothly. Afterwards, the chaplain invited us for coffee and cake at a nearby cafe. I was curious as to what crimes these women had committed. Four had committed domestic violence offenses and eight were mentally ill. Mentally ill and locked up in prison. Confined behind barbed wire, eating starchy food, locked away from their loved ones. What kind of mental help was this? Prison?

My thoughts traveled to the facility my father had lived in. He was surrounded by brilliant green lawns and the sound of birds chirping good morning. Oh, it was still a confined mental health facility, but he was able to access the outdoors when he was on good behavior. He was protected from living on the streets, from being robbed, beaten, or killed. He was cared for and received medication dispensed accurately in a safe haven. He was never able to live on his own. We were protected from his violent outbursts.

We still cared for him; it wasn't as if because he lived there during the week we abandoned our responsibilities. Dad remained a part of our lives until he died. He and his illness never left our psyches.

I remember how resourceful he could be. I had moved two and a half hours north of Milwaukee to a small town. I had taken a second job in a town 19 miles from where I lived. I needed extra money for Christmas presents and worked at a department store. This particular below-zero day I almost didn't go to work for fear my car wouldn't start when I got off at nine o'clock. One of my sons came with me. He looked at all the toys in the store while I worked. It was a small town; you could do that with peace of mind. Upon beginning work I traveled downstairs to pick up my check. In utter disbelief I thought I saw my father standing in line at the courtesy counter. Was I delusional? Rushing to find my son, I said, "Go downstairs and take a look and tell me—is that your grandfather?"

He returned with a big smile and said, "Yes, it is!"

There stood my father in a maroon plaid winter jacket, red muffler wrapped around his neck. Bareheaded, standing patiently in line. My father didn't have any money; he didn't have a car. How in the world could this be? Visions of him not wanting to return to the hospital raced through my mind. Fear creeped down my icy veins. What sort of mood was he in? Why did he come here? How did he get here? How was it even possible that he was downstairs in this store? My hands were shaking when I explained to my boss I had to go home.

"My mentally ill father, who lives in Milwaukee, is standing downstairs," I stammered.

Face pale, I grabbed my coat and my son and located Dad. I ushered him into the car and, still in shock, asked him how he had managed to find his way to Appleton.

He explained that he took the Greyhound bus. He had bummed some money from his twin brother, took the city bus to the Greyhound bus station in downtown Milwaukee, and bought a ticket to Appleton. Arriving in town, he asked directions to the store and walked there from the bus station. He was going to ask at the service counter how he could locate me.

Stunned, I asked him what would have happened had I not been working—I almost didn't come to work that day because it was ten below zero. He answered, without prevarication, that he would have gone to the police station and requested a ride to my house. I had just had a baby, and he wanted to see the little guy. That laid a punch to my stomach. All that planning just to see his newest grandchild! Times like that chipped away at my ice-encased heart.

Of course, we were all in big trouble at the hospital for NOT checking him out. Like, who knew?

There was another incident when I had driven down to Wauwatosa to spend a weekend with my sister and her family. I brought the kids and one of my daughter's friends. Upon entering the house, we were greeted with a thick cloud of smoke concealing the frivolity at hand. I made out the figure of my father and a few other fellas laughing and drinking. Dad was entertaining some of his friends who were patients from the hospital: old, disheveled, grizzly looking friends.

Dumbstruck, I pushed the kids up the stairs and told them to play in a bedroom. I shut the upstairs door before they could ask questions. I went back to the kitchen, trying to figure out what was going on. When my sister arrived home, she went ballistic. It was a hefty walk from the hospital, but remember, Dad was used to spending his days walking. He knew where she kept the liquor, and he was dispensing brandy to his three friends. They were thoroughly enjoying themselves. It was a grand party. Elaine freaked out. Number one, they were drinking; number two, did the hospital know they were all gone?

Arms flailing, she shouted at the top of her lungs, "Out, all of you!" (For a minute I thought she was going to break into her tap-dancing routine). She shepherded them into her car. Elaine was a take-charge kind of gal. That's why my brother and I deferred to her.

When Elaine returned the men to the hospital, the nurse chewed her out for giving them liquor. Of course my sister explained she knew nothing about this lively excursion, and Dad was quarantined for the upcoming weekend.

There were times Elaine discovered that Dad had brought a small empty bottle to her house. He was siphoning liquor from her brandy bottle. When she questioned him about it, he told her, "Oh, those guys back there just want a little drink." She confiscated it.

Sometimes he took onions back to the hospital so the "fellas" could have onion on their hamburgers. Life continued, putting one foot in front of the other. It is what it is!

Recently there was a documentary on TV where a town in Florida is thinking of refurbishing an old building and converting it to a mental health facility where folks can live if they can't be out on their own or with their families. The building was once a psychiatric facility, a place where those with mental illness could live forever or for a year or two. The patients would receive medical care and counseling on how to ease back into society. Many mentally ill folks do not belong in prison. They do need a safe, protected, supervised place to live—somewhere they'd receive managed medical care. How wonderful it would be if this person in Florida successfully creates a safe haven for those who are mentally ill.

What did Reagan save by closing mental health facilities? Money? It still costs the government to place a mentally ill person in prison. Was this a way forward for privatization of prisons? Did he just want someone else to take care of the problem? Was he just shooting from the hip, not thinking through the fiasco he caused?

I get it; many folks think this is not their problem. They don't want their tax dollars going to reinstate mental health facilities. Would you rather have homeless mentally ill people sleeping on the streets and screaming obscenities at you as you walk downtown?

Would you rather just kick them to the curb? The alternative could be a safe environment protecting everyone from their violent outbursts. Let's take a look and see the world in all its imperfection, its messiness. It's time to deal with mental illness and remove the stigma from it. It's an illness just like cancer or any other life-threatening disease. It is everyone's problem, and it's time to reverse the closing of mental health facilities.

President Jimmy Carter, before leaving office, looked at providing federal grants for mental health programs. The next administration never let the programs survive.

I think about families with a mentally ill person and no one to help them. God knows we only began some semblance of a life when my father was committed to the Milwaukee County Mental Health

Hospital. We were all safe. All of us.

What were Reagan's famous words? "Government is not the solution to our problems. Government is the problem." Really? I will always be eternally grateful that the government provided my family a safe haven.

Someone once said, "The way we treat those who are less than us says a lot about who we really are."

Chapter 19

Stitching Frayed Cloth

My father was 76 when he died. My mother was 64 when my father died. One afternoon, I found Momma slouched over the kitchen table, her head in her hands, her brown hair falling over her distressed face.

"I've never been loved," she softly whispered. Her profound statement stopped me in my tracks. I reached for a kitchen chair and sat down.

"What do you mean?" my hand went to my mouth, my lips quivering in shock.

Briefly she looked up at me. "Today on the bus, I looked across the aisle. There was an elderly couple from India. They sat very quietly. She was wrapped in a beautiful sapphire sari; her head rested on her husband's shoulder. I watched as he softly stroked the side of her cheek, readjusting her headpiece that had slipped backwards. I felt a stab in my stomach watching so much love being displayed."

Momma turned her head to look out the kitchen window, remembering something she had seen in Jacobus Park. "Yesterday I was walking among the fallen leaves in the park," she continued, tears forming in her eyes. "I needed to rest for a minute, so I sat down by the pond. There was a young couple sitting on a bench near me. Their little one was throwing leaves into the pond. As they sat together, the woman watched her child while her husband reached over and took hold of a strand of her long black hair. He twisted it around and around his finger as if he was reliving a special moment, his eyes looking dreamily at his wife. They radiated so much love I had to stifle my cries. The realization hit me: I've never been loved. I've been a married widow all my life. I've never had a life."

I was speechless. Stunned by her epiphany, her realization of what she had missed after all these years numbed my brain. We never considered how lonely she must have been.

"But we love you, Momma, Elaine, Dick and I," I sputtered, groping for words.

"Yes, I know," she sadly smiled. "You kids have been the best part of my life."

We sat in silence for a while. She registered the impact of a loveless marriage. I was struck dumb as reality came crashing into the room.

Her words brought forth a memory of a friend's realization about her lonely marriage. She had revealed to me that when the dentist held her head, preparing her for a procedure, she felt stirred by such a tender moment, a gentle hand on her face. I've never forgotten her sad disclosure. Do we ever really listen when someone pours out their heart? Do we feel the sorrow they are trying to convey to us?

For so long my siblings and I believed that our mother knew what her life was and wasn't, and that she made the most of it. We admired her for her strength and tenacity. I guess we took for granted that she persevered and didn't look back. Now she was looking back. Her woeful revelations seized my mind.

Once, when asked to introduce Momma, I said, "My mother was walking down a path, when everyone was looking one way while she looked the other way. There on the path lay some rose-colored glasses. She reached down and put them on, and when she did, she no longer saw the world in black and gray." Often, I would argue with her, "Momma, you never see the black and gray in life."

She'd reply, "Yes, Kathleen"—she always called me that—"but you don't see the rainbows." The rainbows ended that day in the kitchen. How was she able to hold the black and gray at bay for so many years?

Momma was right, though; life had thrown her a yakker. In the beginning of their relationship, how was she to know that Dad was mentally ill? How does anyone know the medical condition beforehand of someone who glides you across the dance floor? What surprises are lurking in the darkness? You're in the middle of a heated encounter when you pull away and say, "Just a minute before we continue; let's take a look at your health record and family history."

The recollection of those long-ago romantic encounters brought some color to her cheeks.

I went on, "In high school I had a teacher who was always dispensing philosophy. He told us the best marriages are those made in high school. You've spent years together; you know the ins and outs of the other person's personality; you probably know the family and parent situation also." A vision of our neighborhood bully passed through my mind, and I wondered who had been silly enough to marry him.

I guess naiveté is what keeps species reproducing when maybe they shouldn't.

Now life was revealed in a very strong way. I reminded Momma what a rock she had been. What a wonderful life she had carved out for us kids and herself in such difficult situations—the constant stability she presented to us. I told her how she never seemed consumed with depression. (Well, maybe, that one Christmas when she sat by her sewing machine in a paralyzed stupor and I offered to wrap everyone's Christmas gifts without peeking at any. Other than that one episode, she either hid her depressive feelings or moved through them.)

Momma's strong character permeated our bones. We pushed through challenges, denying negativity to overcome any situation. To this day, my sister and I have little tolerance for weak women. I can't stand a novel featuring a weak female character. Under Momma's tutelage, we learned responsibility. She taught us compassion entwined with power, a velvet hammer.

I had to begin somewhere, so I stammered, "Remember how terrified you were to fly? When I became a stewardess, I told you I had free passes to fly on Continental. Use them!

"You boarded a jet by yourself. When you arrived in Houston at 11:30 p.m., I met you at the airport and told you to keep your suitcase—we're leaving on the midnight flight to Denver. I had requested a transfer from a difficult supervisor, and my transfer was approved at midnight. We flew together to Denver and stayed in a motel. Your introduction to flight awakened dormant desires for adventure."

A thin smile creeped across her saddened face.

"Not long after that you became a jetsetter, flying to Denver on the weekend, and back to work Sunday evening. There was no stopping you. Your love of travel inspired trips to visit German relatives. If that wasn't enough, you arranged European trips with inexperienced gals from work. An encouraging example smoothing the way for frightened women. I never thought I'd see the day with you riding an elephant in Egypt, and that was after you had hip surgery! In Austria you grabbed someone's Austrian hat and joined in their small-town parade, much to the chagrin of our German aunts.

"It didn't take long for you to lend a hand to impecunious Marquette college students unable to afford a wedding reception. With your, 'I could do it for you' attitude, their wedding dinner was whipped up for a fraction of the cost. I think you were lucky if you charged enough to cover food expenses. This passion led to you create a small catering business using the industrial church kitchen. Using the church kitchen came about from an article I wrote in the *Milwaukee Journal*. The article told of how you created this small business from your home, which brought a visit from the health department. Oops! Using your home kitchen to sell food is frowned upon.

"Your grandchildren were the recipients of a memorable Christmas Eve celebration at your house, complete with a visit from Santa Claus and, of course, Billie the Brownie. These treasured memories are stored lovingly in all their minds.

"Even though Dad could mess up a lovely evening, you didn't let it stop you from entertaining. Elaine, Dick, and I always looked forward to when it was your turn to host a Cousin Club party. We assisted in bringing out the good china and covering card tables with colorful cross-stitched tablecloths. There was such a sense of bonhomie when you were all together. Who could forget your famous sandwich loaf: one part egg salad, one part olive spread, one part ham salad, all frosted in cream cheese and rolled in nuts. Of course there were brandy Old Fashioneds that got the gals rollicky. Cards were played for nickels—something called 'Two to the right, one to the left.' Our living room was alive with your gaiety, cloaking all adversity.

"What a determined role model you are. You honored your obligations to raising us with what little we had. We barely knew we were poor. Your strength taught us to never wallow in self-pity. These were just some of the lessons you conveyed to us.

"I remember you telling me when we flew to Germany, 'Here I am, the poorest of my family, and I'm the first to meet grandma's relatives!' A smile encompassed your face."

To myself I was thinking, "It's too late now to lament on things you never had." I didn't say that, though; her words had my stomach churning. Problems, always more problems this life kept pitching to us. I had images of her wanting someone to tenderly hold her, to fill her nights with gentle affection. The love she thought was promised had been short lived.

Momma was a formidable woman who reluctantly accepted the challenge of loneliness, braved the unknown, and shouldered on.

Then, just like in the movies, a young 70-year-old with love on his mind had his eyes on this lovely, graceful gal. Pulling back his shoulders to make himself visible, he began volunteering in the church kitchen where Momma was stirring up some luscious chocolate cakes. Dates followed—those famous Friday night Milwaukee fish fries, ending with an evening of dancing. Another great dancer! Go figure! Maybe this time she'd waltz to a happier tune. Dance was awakening dormant feelings.

119

One lovely fall day, I had an unexpected surprise. Living two and a half hours north of Milwaukee, I was greeted with a door flung open. "Hi, is anyone home?" Just my Momma and her beau, Art, bouncing through the front door, pointing a sparkling ring finger toward me. Time teaches you to make hay while the sun shines, and they listened!

In 1985, Momma and Art were married at a lovely church wedding, surrounded by giddy relatives and family. My brother Dick beamed as Best Man, and I was the grateful Matron of Honor. A raucous old-fashioned German reception lifted everyone's spirits.

My heart stirred at the beginning strands of the song, "May I have this dance for the rest of my life, Will you be my partner every day?" The words penetrated my soul. This song remains synonymous with my mother's wedding. Her new husband walked across the dance floor, his eyes overflowing with love. Art enfolded her in his arms as they gracefully circled the dance floor. Momma floated past me in her violet crepe dress, white orchids pinned to her ample bosom, "something old" shoes on her feet. She glowed like a Cheshire cat. Loneliness seemed to evaporate with each dance step.

They were engulfed in applause. His smile conveyed, "I've got the most beautiful gal in the room. Do not cut in." It was Momma's time in the well-deserved limelight. Here came her rainbows again. My heart was pounding out messages: thank you, thank you, for the love my mother was now receiving. Thoughts of, "Please God, let her have it right this time," thundered in my head.

I felt shivers running up and down my arms; a happy ache grabbed my stomach. I hoped this moment would erase the pain she had endured. The sight of the two of them reawakened my appreciation of how good life can be. The glow of their faces sent ripples of relief through my body.

Momma was surrounded by a shimmering aura. A knowing smile shone in her soft brown eyes. I wondered if she would have made different choices knowing the pain life would bring. Would she have reached out to assist others in need had her life been more normal, whatever normal is? Would there still have been empathy for others?

For now, all I cared about was that my mother was being adored by a man oozing with kindness. This was her time to be adored, a time to feel special. It was a fairy tale after all, with challenges met and love waiting in the wings. But life can be unfair. You get what you get and somehow you must make it fit.

Later on in life, she winked at her granddaughter and told her, "The sex was good, too!"

Chapter 20

Life's Lessons Learned

It's autumn in the Rockies—rivers of aspen gold cascade down the sides of the mountains. Soon the peaks will be blanketed with champagne powder beckoning eager skiers to the slopes.

I wonder what my father would have thought had he been able to experience the splendor of the Rocky Mountains. Would he have broken out in song?

His condition taught me over and over, "You get what you get, and somehow you must make it fit!"

My mother taught me to look for the rainbows.

And my great-grandfather's words, "It's easier to laugh, rather than cry, and oh, so much more comfortable," are always resonating with me.

Tante Anna taught me to remember that when things go wrong, now you have a story to tell.

Without the help of others, rainbows and laughter remain elusive.

We are not in this world alone; we are all a part of one. Maybe we just need to be reminded not to look away when life gets messy.

We need each other as we travel through this journey of life.

Family Photos

Great-Great-Grandfather
Georg Geuder

Great-Great-Grandmother
Louisa Stern

Great-Grandparents **William Geuder** and **Emma Paeschke**

Geuder, Paeschke & Frey Manufacturing Company

William Geuder (top left), **Tante Anna** (top right),
George Geuder (lower right), and sisters.

Grandparents **George Geuder**
and Elizabeth **Zeidler**
Baby **George** on the left,
William on the right.

William Geuder (top left)
George Geuder (2nd row, 2nd from left)

Hawley Road Kindergarten
William Geuder (top row, 4th from right),
George Geuder (1st row, 1st on right)

Grandmother
Elizabeth Kranz Schlenvogt
on her wedding day.

Grandparents **Elizabeth** and
Emil Schleinvogt.

My mother, **Olga Schleinvogt**
—high school graduation.

129

Hawley Road Elementary Kindergarten
Kathleen (Kady) Geuder (3rd row, 5th from left)

**The Geuders: Olga, William,
Elaine, Kathleen (Kady) and Dick**

Tante Anna

Cousin Club
Olga Geuder (1st row, 1st on the left)
Tante Anna (2nd row, 1st on left)

Dress up day at work. **Olga Geuder** (1st on right)

Dick and **Rex.**

Art and **Olga Peterson**'s wedding dance.

Kady loved her cut-outs!

Acknowledgements

We need the help of others as we travel through and try to unravel this great mystery called life. We are all a part of each other.

To my son **Michael Martin**, I say thank you. Your insights to my story provided me with revelations of how certain folks were important in my life, and how those folks enhanced and enriched my life with moments of joy. Your inquisitive mind inspired me to delve deeper. Your unlimited time and expertise made this book possible. It proved again that old adage, "When the pupil is ready, the teacher will come!"!

To **Hilde Cytryn**, who shared her laughter and wine, enhancing many a dull work gathering and continuing our friendship over the years, thank you. Your reading and rereading of my manuscript emboldened me to carry on. Your suggestions improved and strengthened my story. I am deeply indebted to your powerful love.

To Hilda's son, **Steven**, who not only took time to read my manuscript, but offered to purchase my first copy. You brought tears to my eyes. Thank you.

To **Patti Gassaway**, my sincere gratitude for your multiple readings of this manuscript and for fortifying my courage to carry on. Thank you!

To **my daughter Jennifer Martin**, who graciously added her succinct memories of her grandfather and her strong support as she edited pages and pages. You enhanced my story tenfold. Thank you.

To my son, **Tom Martin**, who over the years shared his spiritual quest with me. His gentle critique of my story pushed me forward. Thank you!

To **Cathy Martin**, my daughter in love, thank you so much for the beautiful book cover you designed. You have given me a great gift.

To my son **Chris Martin**, who helps me in ways he doesn't even realize and fills my heart with gratitude I say, thank you!

To **Stephanie Martin**, my daughter in love, who is my biggest cheerleader and spent hours editing this story. Thank you for always lifting my spirits.

To my daughter in love **Sally Martin**, who makes me feel good with her uplifting, forthright British charm, thank you.

To my special grandchildren, **Abby and Evan Martin**, who sustain me with their lovely texts to Grandma, a BIG THANK YOU!

To **Maggie Wohlberg**, who graciously read my manuscript and shared her stories with me, thank you.

To **Renee Christian**, who shared her table at the Boulder farmers market and ended up reading my manuscript. Thank you so very much!

To my cousins **Maxine Dodge, Cathy Hewitt, Luanne Mazzone, Pat Schmidt, Jim Biancalana**, and **Marge Zeidler**, thank you, thank you for sharing your memories. We had some fun and crazy times.

To **MaryAnn Widerman**, though our weekly luncheons could include unexpected chaos, your eye-opening writing tips moved my story forward. Thank you.

To **Amy Hyder,** for your talented editing skills and generous personality, thank you.

To **Nelson Gurda** and **Thomas Mitchell**, who are overcoming obstacles of their own and still encouraging others, I say thank you!

For **Lu Nosziko**: although small in stature, she was a force to be reckoned with and generous with her love and advice. Love always.

To **Harriet Freiberger**, from the Steamboat writer's group, a friend and enthusiastic, positive force in my life, I can't thank you enough.

To **my husband Marty**, who drew a meticulous family tree and provided three hots and a well-used cot, thank you.

To songwriters and musicians everywhere, thank you for sharing your love of words and filling the world with your melodic sounds. The music you create, notes that uplift and penetrate our souls, take the edge off life; a heartfelt thank you. Especially thank you to Kris Kristofferson, a prolific songwriter whose music helped me make it through many a night.

And to **my sister Elaine**, it's time for us to tell our secret. Thank you for your love and support over the years. Now aren't you glad you didn't trade me for those darling twins? Who would have written this story?

Credits

"The Voyagers: A History of the Geuders
and Paeschkes, 1600-1940"

Translated letters sent to Kathy Martin
from cousin Margaret Engelke

GPF History Brochure

Salon article on Ronald Reagan's shameful legacy,
September 29, 2013

Paramount Walking Tour of Grafton, Wisconsin Brochure

"Schuster's and Gimbels," by Paul H. Geenen

Edited by Michael Martin

Cover art by Cathy Martin

Book design by Beth Foster,
Pinecone Book Company

About the Author

Kathleen "Kady" Geuder Martin grew up in Milwaukee, Wisconsin. Her heartfelt memories of delectable frozen custard, Karl Rausch's savory potato dumplings, oom-pah-pah, polkas, Cousin Clubs, Friday night fish fries, studying for finals at Bradford Beach, and trips Up North linger on. Her roots are steeped in Milwaukee's political and manufacturing history. In later life Kady moved to a small Northern Wisconsin town. Her restless spirit connected with a dynamic YWCA director in Appleton, Wisconsin. They hatched a plan taking Kady's talent in a new direction. For the next 40 years, Kady became the Pied Piper of storytelling performances at schools, libraries, churches, civic clubs, and scouting events around the state of Wisconsin. Her children assisted but soon were replaced by children in the audience clamoring to be a part of the program. Her children's storybook, *I Hate to Wait!*, is an audience participatory book. Kady went on to publish a children's party book, *Party Shakers*, and a family party book, *Let's Party*. A participatory story video, *Tell A Tale*, is popular with preschools, elementary schools, and parents. Kady published articles in *Good Housekeeping*, *Modern Maturity*, and regional magazines. She resides in Denver, Colorado with her husband and golden retriever.

Made in United States
Troutdale, OR
08/05/2023

11832810R00094